Beyond the University

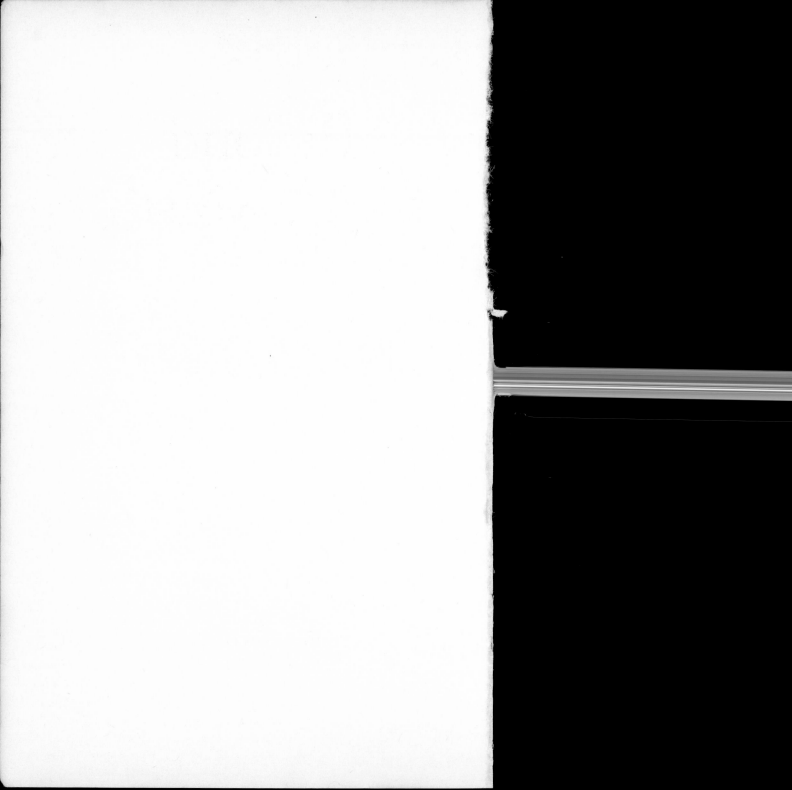

Beyond the University

Why Liberal Education Matters

■

MICHAEL S. ROTH

With a New Preface

Yale

UNIVERSITY PRESS

NEW HAVEN AND LONDON

Published with assistance from the foundation established in memory
of Calvin Chapin of the Class of 1788, Yale College.

Yale University Press books may be purchased in quantity for
educational, business, or promotional use. For information, please
e-mail sales.press@yale.edu (U.S. office) or sales@yaleup.co.uk
(U.K. office).

Set in Electra type by IDS Infotech, Ltd.
Printed in the United States of America.

Library of Congress Control Number: 2015933205
ISBN 978-0-300-21266-2 (pbk.)

A catalogue record for this book is available from the British Library.

10 9 8 7 6 5 4 3 2 1

For my teachers and my students

Contents

Preface to the Paperback Edition

▪

SINCE BEYOND THE UNIVERSITY was first published, I've been talking with groups across the country about the challenges facing American higher education. I've also talked with thousands of young people trying to plan their paths beyond high school in a context of increasing costs, debt, and doubts about the efficacy of traditional undergraduate learning. While acknowledging the dynamics of cultural and economic change, I continue to urge all concerned to consider college not just as a chance to acquire particular expertise but as a remarkable opportunity to explore their individual and social lives in connection to the world in which they will live and work.

As I show in this book, contentious debates over the benefits — or drawbacks — of broad, integrative learning, liberal learning, are as old as America itself. Several of the founding fathers saw education as the road to independence and liberty. A broad commitment to inquiry was part of their dedication to freedom. But critics of education also have a long tradition. From Benjamin Franklin in the eighteenth century to today's Internet pundits, they have attacked its irrelevance and elitism, often calling for more vocational instruction.

Ben Franklin probably would have had some sympathy for the anti-college message: "You don't need colleges. Go off and learn stuff on your own. You believe you are an innovator? You can prove it without the sheepskin. You want to start a successful company? You don't need permission from out-of-touch professors." From Thomas Paine to Steve Jobs, stories of people with the smarts and chutzpah to educate themselves in their own ways have long resonated with Americans.

But Franklin was also dismissive of the arrogant display of parochialism. He would be appalled by the current mania for driving young people into narrower and narrower domains in the name of "day one" job preparedness. He would surely recognize that when industrial and civic leaders call for earlier and earlier specialization, they are putting us on a path that will make Americans even less capable citizens who are less able to adjust to changes in the world of work.

Citizens able to see through political or bureaucratic double-talk are also workers who can defend their rights in the face of the rich and powerful. Education protects against mindless tyranny and haughty privilege.

Would-be reformers of education have long adopted instrumentalist rhetoric to argue for the irrelevance of what goes on at campuses—from laboratories to libraries. Today conservative scholars like Charles Murray, Richard Vedder, and Peter Wood ask why people destined for low-paying jobs should bother to pursue their education beyond high school, much less study philosophy, literature, and history. The venture capitalist Peter Thiel has offered money to would-be entrepreneurs to quit college and focus on Web-based start-ups instead. Business-school gurus like Clayton Christensen tell us that "disruptive innovation" is causing liberal arts learning to be "disintermediated" so as to deliver just what the "end user" needs. From this narrow, instrumentalist perspective, students are consumers buying a customized playlist of knowledge.

Some of the language of this critique may be new, but the call for a more narrowly tailored education — especially for Americans with limited economic prospects — is not. A century ago, organizations as varied as chambers of commerce and labor federations backed plans for a dual system of teaching, wherein some students would be trained for specific occupations, while others would get a broad education allowing them to continue their studies in college. As I discuss in chapter 4 of this book, this movement led to the Smith-Hughes Act of 1917, which financed vocational education, initially for jobs in agriculture and then in other industries.

The philosopher John Dewey, America's most influential thinker on education, opposed this effort. Though he was open to integrating manual training into school curriculums, Dewey opposed the dual-track system because he recognized that it would reinforce the inequalities of his time. Wouldn't such a system have the same result today?

To be sure, Dewey recognized the necessity of gainful employment. "The world in which most of us live is a world in which everyone has a calling and occupation, something to do," he wrote in *The School and Society*. "Some are managers and others are subordinates. But the great thing for one as for the other is that each shall have had the education which enables him to see within his daily work all there is in it of large and human significance."

Education should aim to enhance our capacities, Dewey argued, so that we are not reduced to mere tools. "The kind of vocational education in which I am interested is not one which will 'adapt' workers to the existing industrial regime; I am not sufficiently in love with the regime for that." Are we?

Who wants to attend school to learn to be "human capital" for the latest investment schemes? Who really aspires for their children to become mere resources for somebody else's purpose? Dewey had a different vision. Given the pace of change, it is impossible (he noted in 1897) to know what the world will be like in a couple of decades, so schools first and foremost should teach us habits of learning.

For Dewey, these habits included not just reliance on one's own thinking but also awareness of our interdependence; nobody is an expert on everything. In *Democracy and Education*, he emphasized "plasticity," an openness to being shaped by experience: "The inclination to learn from life itself and to make the conditions of life such that all will learn in the process of living is the finest product of schooling."

The inclination to learn from life can be taught in a traditional liberal arts curriculum, but also in schools that focus on real-world skills, from engineering to nursing. The key is to develop habits of mind that allow students to keep learning even as they acquire skills to get things done. This combination—what I call pragmatic liberal education—will serve students as individuals, family members, and citizens—not just as employees and managers.

Higher education today faces stark challenges: the ravaging of public universities' budgets by strained state and local governments, ever rising tuition and student debt, inadequate student achievement, the corrosive impact of soaring inequality, and some elite institutions' neglect of their core mission of teaching undergraduates.

But these problems, however urgent, should not cause us to neglect Dewey's insight that learning in the process of living is the deepest form of freedom. In a nation that aspires to democracy, that's what education is primarily for: the cultivation of freedom within society. We should not think of schools as training camps to prepare us to step into a narrow function defined by someone else. Rather, higher education's highest purpose is to give all citizens the opportunity to find "large and human significance" in their lives and work.

As I describe in *Beyond the University*, liberal learning in the American tradition isn't only training; it's an invitation to think for oneself in a context of interdependence. For generations of Americans, literate and well-rounded citizens were seen as essential to a healthy republic.

Broadly educated citizens aren't just collections of skills—they are whole people. However, for today's critics, often speaking the lingo of Silicon Valley sophistication, a broad, contextual education is merely wasted—non-monetized—schooling.

It's no wonder that in a society characterized by radical income inequality, anxiety about getting that first job leads many to aim for the immediate needs of the marketplace. The high cost of college and the ruinous debt that many take on only add to this anxiety. In this context, some assert that education should simply prepare people to be consumers, or, if they are talented enough, innovators. But when the needs of the market change, as they surely will, the folks with that narrow training will be out of luck. Their bosses, those responsible for defining market trends, will be just fine because they were probably never confined to such an ultra-specialized way of doing things. Beware of critics of education who cloak their desire to protect privilege (and inequality) in the garb of educational reform.

"If we make money the object of man-training," W. E. B. Du Bois wrote in "The Talented Tenth" at the beginning of the twentieth century, "we shall develop money makers but not necessarily men." He went on to describe how "intelligence, broad sympathy, knowledge of the world that was and is, and the relation of men to it—this is the curriculum of that Higher Education which must underlie true life." A good pragmatist, Du Bois knew that through education one develops modes of thinking that turn into patterns of action. As William James taught, the point of learning is not to arrive at truths that somehow match up with reality. The point of learning is to acquire better ways of coping with the world, better ways of acting.

Better ways of acting were the focus of Jane Addams's efforts, and she built a cooperative practice of teaching and learning that addressed the needs of some of our most vulnerable citizens. Addams's love of learning was deep, but she became convinced that education wasn't a spectator sport. School shouldn't deaden in us the ability to respond to others; it should enhance that ability. She knew that colleges were guiding students toward what the pragmatists called "habits of action." Educational institutions had the obligation to turn their graduates away from arrogant egotism and toward an engagement that could make a positive difference in society and culture.

Pragmatic liberal education in America aims to empower students with potent ways of dealing with the issues they will face at work and in life. That's why it must be broad and contextual, exploring interconnections and inspiring habits of attention and critique that will be resources for students years after graduation. In order to develop this resource, teachers must address the student as a whole person, not just as a tool kit that can be improved. We all do need tools, to be sure, but American college education has long invited students to learn to learn, creating habits of independent critical and creative thinking that last a lifetime.

In the nineteenth century, Ralph Waldo Emerson urged students to "resist the vulgar prosperity that retrogrades ever to barbarism." He emphasized that a true education would help one find one's own way by expanding one's world, not by narrowing it: notice everything but imitate nothing, he urged. The goal of this cultivated attentiveness is not to discover some ultimate Truth, but neither is it just to prepare for the worst job one is likely to ever have, one's first job after graduation.

Instead, the goal of liberal education is, in John Dewey's words, "to free experience from routine and caprice." This goal will make one more effective in the world, and it will help one continue to grow as a whole person beyond the university. This project, like learning itself, should never end.

Acknowledgments

IN MY FIRST year as a college student, I often said I couldn't understand why somebody would study something just to teach it to somebody else. By the time I finished my undergraduate degree, I found that I enjoyed reading and research so much that I had a hard time imagining a future without further studies. My priority was to continue my education. I was very fortunate to have attended an extraordinarily intense yet open small university, Wesleyan, and then to go on to graduate work at Princeton. Both schools encouraged invigorating cultures of inquiry, and my teachers were very willing to let me follow my interests. I continued to wonder whether I should be studying philosophy, history, or psychology (I turned down a job in a psychiatric hospital to attend a Ph.D. program in history). My teachers basically said to stop worrying about what to call my field and to go to the classes that interested me while pursuing my research projects. I needed, they stressed, to continue my education. Eventually concluding that I was "focused" on how people make sense of the past, I did complete a Ph.D. in history. But my first book was on psychoanalysis (based on my senior thesis at Wesleyan) and my dissertation was on the history of philosophy. I was eventually a history and humanities professor before running a research program (and doing some curatorial work) at the Getty Research Institute for the History of Art. I went on to be president of California College of the Arts before returning to Wesleyan as president. It was good not to have to make up my mind. It still is.

I had remarkably gifted teachers at Wesleyan and Princeton—teachers who provided guidance and inspiration, mixed with more than a little discipline and critique. I loved my teachers, but I didn't know that I would love teaching. Then, when given the opportunity to run discussion seminars in graduate school, I emerged giddy with excitement. "I can't believe they pay us for this," I would exclaim—to the chagrin of my fellow T.A.s, who pointed out how little they in fact paid us. I discovered that working with students on topics I cared about was going to be one of the joys of my life.

And what wonderful students I've had at Scripps College, Claremont Graduate University, California College of the Arts, and now back at Wesleyan! And in the last year I've had the dizzying and ultimately fulfilling experience of teaching online. My Coursera class is very different from the courses at the small institutions at which I've worked, but the energy of learning and the self-transformation that the students report have been stimulating and gratifying.

As a teacher, whether in the classroom or online, I devote much time to quoting texts. I want my classes to discover the joys of paying attention to the language, structure, and layered meanings in the books we read together. In this book, too, I provide more than the usual amount of quotations. I am hopeful that readers will get a feel for the compelling voices in the rich and varied American tradition of liberal education and that some will turn back to this tradition for further study (and pleasure).

I dedicate this book to my teachers and my students. They have allowed me to continue my education through more than three decades.

■

In the last few years, I have had several opportunities to try out some of the ideas expressed in this book with different audiences. I am grateful to the institutions at which I've lectured on liberal education and to the publications in which I've explored some of these ideas (*Chronicle for Higher Education, Huffington Post, Inside Higher Ed, Los Angeles Times, New York Times, Wall Street Journal, Washington Post*). My trustee, faculty, and administrative colleagues at Wesleyan have heard me out on the issues discussed in this book, and they have responded—often quite vigorously. I am grateful for their patience, insights, and dedication.

The staff of the President's Office at Wesleyan has been enormously helpful to me throughout the time I've worked on this volume. Joan Adams, Marianne Calnen, Heather Brooke, and Lisa LaPlant have given me the time and space to write. Andy Tanaka has helped me oversee every sector of university operations so that I can also have the opportunity to turn to research and writing. These are great gifts.

The talented editor Ileene Smith and I first discussed this project when she was working with Yale University Press, and I am very grateful to her for her insights. Ileene introduced me to Georges Borchardt, who is now my agent. Georges's serene, intelligent responsiveness has helped keep this book on track. Steve Wasserman, who first gave me assignments (and advice) many years ago when he was at the *Los Angeles Times Book Review*, has seen the book through as an editor at Yale. I am grateful for his constructive input.

For many years now, Charles Salas has read my work with the intention of making it clearer, more accessible, and less prone to error. This has taken much time and effort. Although we agree there is more to be done, I want to express my deep thanks.

I've written this book sitting side by side with Kari Weil, my wife and colleague. While writing her own book (and essays, lectures, and student evaluations), she has suffered through my attempts to say something about psychoanalysis, history, photography, crafts, film, philosophy, and now education. Her critical acumen is exceeded only by her sweet, empathic energies, and I have been the lucky recipient of both. Without her, I'd never have gotten beyond the university.

Introduction

∎

WHEN I BEGAN my freshman year at Wesleyan University almost forty years ago, I had only the vaguest notion of what a liberal education was. My father (like his father before him) was a furrier, and my mother sang with a big band before she decided to start a family. Giving their children access to a college education was part of their American dream, even if campuses sometimes seemed to them like foreign countries. Now I serve as president of the same institution at which they first dropped me off, and where I stumbled into courses like Intro to Philosophy and Abnormal Psychology. Much has changed in higher education since my student days. At highly selective schools, many undergraduates now behave like consumers, arriving on campuses with specific demands and detailed plans for their eight semesters. Many are intent on building résumés by choosing to double-major and accumulate credentials to match what they imagine to be an employer's expectations. Parents check that the facilities of the institution meet their standards of comfort and sophistication and want to be reassured that their student will develop specific skills that will justify the extraordinary financial investment that many private colleges and universities require. At large public institutions, declining state support has led to massive over-crowding, faculty who are underpaid and often part-time, and a creeping culture of pessimism about the quality of undergraduate learning. Students often enter the university system without the preparation to complete college-level classes, and professors are caught between maintaining standards and meeting the needs of undergraduates whose reading and math skills are woefully inadequate. A vast number of students drop out within the first two years, and those who persevere often have trouble completing their degrees because of the limited number of open seats in required classes.

Given this context, a broad education that sets the foundation for a lifetime of learning can seem impossibly idealistic. These days the words "college education" are more likely to be linked to the words "excessive debt" than "liberal learning." Parents want their children's education to be immediately useful, and with a dramatically shrink-ing job market, undergrads themselves are often eager to follow a straight and narrow path that they imagine will land them that coveted first job. A broad liberal arts educa-tion, with a significant opportunity to explore oneself and the world, is increasingly seen as a luxury for the entitled, one that is scarcely affordable in a hypercompetitive world.

Beyond the University argues that the demand that we replace broad contextual education meant to lead to lifelong learning with targeted vocational undergraduate instruction is a critical mistake, one that neglects a deep American tradition of humanistic education that has been integral to our success as a nation and that has enriched the lives of generations of students by enhancing their capacities for shaping themselves and reinventing the world they will inhabit. Since the founding of this country, ideas of education have been closely tied to individual freedom and hope for the future—to thinking for oneself and contributing to society by unleashing one's creative potential. Building on this tradition, in the twentieth century the American pragmatists developed ideas of experience and inquiry that serve personal and civic life without being narrowly utilitarian. Access to a broad, self-critical and pragmatic education has been and remains essential for a culture that prizes innovation and an economy that depends on it. It also remains essential for a society that aspires to being democratic.

Of course, liberal education is not just an American idea. The roots of the concept extend back to the ancient world, and they grew into enduring institutions in the Middle Ages. In Western traditions going back to the Greeks, a "liberal" education was to be liberating, requiring freedom to study and aiming at freedom through understanding. The medieval emphasis on the seven liberal arts (grammar, logic, rhetoric, arithmetic, geometry, music, and astronomy) pictured all of them within a framework set either by philosophy/theology or by rhetoric/oratory. Although today in education we tend to emphasize the legacies of the philosophic ideas of inquiry (think

Socratic method), for centuries education had been conceptualized as the deepening appreciation of great cultural achievements. This was a rhetorical tradition into which one was initiated so as to learn the virtues associated with a canon of monumental works—not a philosophical commitment to discover truths. Several recent commentators on liberal education have emphasized how the philosophical and rhetorical traditions have uneasily coexisted in an American context, especially with respect to the humanities.[1] The philosophical thread is skeptical, focused on inquiry and critical thinking. The rhetorical thread is reverential, focused on bringing new members into the common culture. The threads have been woven together in a variety of ways, giving rise to educational patterns that serve the "whole person"—to use a phrase popular in contemporary Chinese discussions of liberal learning.[2] At least since the eighteenth-century Enlightenment, these patterns have been significantly reconfigured in the West, not least because of the challenges that the sciences posed to either a theologically or a classically oriented education. Inquiry and critique replaced religion and knowledge of ancient languages as hallmarks of the modern research university that spread from Germany to America in the late nineteenth century. This paradigm of the research university has shaped higher education practices until our own day, though the reverential, rhetorical tradition persists, especially in core curricula at the undergraduate level.

Liberal education, as I use the term throughout this book, refers to the combination of the philosophical and rhetorical traditions of how one learns as a whole person. In contemporary higher education, the philosophical tradition has resulted in an emphasis on inquiry and critical thinking—learning to develop as an autonomous person by shedding illusions and acquiring knowledge through research. But a spirit of critique is only one aspect of a well-rounded education, and its overemphasis can lead to sterility rather than creativity.[3] Modern universities that foster liberal education also depend on the rhetorical tradition, which has come to frame how students learn to appreciate or to participate in traditions of compelling cultural interest. This framework helps students understand their connections with others and with canonical works in religion, art, literature, science, and music (to name just some strands of cultural interest). Liberal education intertwines the philosophical and rhetorical so that we learn how to learn, so that we continue both inquiry and cultural participation throughout our lives because learning has become part of who we are.

This book looks back through American history at thinkers whose ideas on education can still inspire us today. Although the focus is American, the ideas developed here have been important to discussions of education throughout the world—from democratic and anticolonial movements to recent efforts to capture creativity and entrepreneurship. We begin with Thomas Jefferson, who saw education as the key preparation for citizens and as an important weapon in fighting the abuses of wealth and privilege. "Preach," he wrote, "a crusade against ignorance; establish and improve the law for educating the common people."[4] The health of a republic, he argued, depends on the education of its citizens. In founding the University of Virginia, he emphasized the freedom that students and faculty would exercise there. Unlike Harvard and its many imitators, he said, Virginia would *not* prescribe a course of study to direct graduates to "the particular vocations to which they are destined."[5] Jefferson had a broader view of educational purpose for the individual and society, a view that has continued to inform our approach to the college years despite calls for more vocationally tailored training.

Jefferson knew that as members of an educated citizenry we are better able to recognize and overcome our distance from—our strangeness to—one another. We learn to recognize that people and ideas that at first seem foreign may indeed have much to teach us. William James would later describe this "overcoming blindness" and remembering to look for the "whole inward significance" of another's situation as crucial dimensions of an education that takes us beyond the borders of our own comfort zones. A liberal education, Ralph Waldo Emerson said, should deepen our ability to "animate" dimensions of the world around us (aspects of nature, culture, enterprise) and not just to criticize them. Emerson wrote that colleges "serve us, when they aim not to drill, but to create; when they gather from far every ray of various genius to their hospitable halls, and, by the concentrated fires, set the hearts of their youth on flame."[6] Liberal education teaches us to open ourselves to the world's "various genius" and to ignite our own and perhaps someone else's imagination. Jane Addams emphasized the challenges and the opportunities for using one's education to deepen one's empathy, to expand the sympathetic imagination. At its best, education develops the capacities for seeing possibilities and for relishing the world across borders we might otherwise not have dared to cross. Education must lead us beyond these borders if it is to be more than training for a role that has already been allocated to us by the powers that be. By expanding our horizons, liberal learning gives us a context for hope, and it requires some confidence in the future. As Dewey put it, to discover "what one is fitted to do, and to secure an opportunity to do it, is the key to happiness."[7] Rather than starting out with a predetermined outcome for what students must do, liberal education helps them make those discoveries and secure those opportunities.

The commitment to liberal learning that Jefferson described has been attacked for its potential elitism and irrelevance for more than two hundred years. It has also been cherished by generations of students and teachers, and many of the best high school graduates still compete for the chance to pursue this education at highly selective institutions. In the last few years, commentators (who usually themselves have had a liberal education) have again questioned whether we should encourage so many people to have the opportunity to make this discovery. Economists have recently queried whether it's worth it for mail carriers, for example, to have spent time and money in learning about the world and themselves when they could have been saving for a house. Sociologists have wondered if by increasing access to college we are creating inappropriate expectations for a workforce that will not regularly be asked to tap into a capacity for independent judgment and critical thinking. Many complain about the cost of a liberal education, about its disconnect from the real world, about its elitism and its political correctness. Pundits write that we must make it more relevant while politicians growl about making it more efficient. The complaints of recent years are not that different from those that Jefferson faced when he described his plans for the University of Virginia, or the ones my parents heard when they decided that their children should go to college. Liberal education will always arouse such criticism in a land driven by economic ambition and anxiety, even more so today when hope for the future has come to seem so tenuous. If higher education is conceived only as a job-placement program for positions with which we are already familiar, then liberal learning does not make much sense. But if higher education is to be an intellectual and experiential adventure and not a bureaucratic assignment of skill capacity, if it is to prize free inquiry rather than training for "the specific vocations to which [students] are destined," then we must resist the call to limit access to it or to diminish its scope.

Beyond the University consists of four chapters: The first describes the deep commitment to liberal learning in the United States from the time of its founding. Jefferson argued for the necessity of a broad education in our young Republic, and African American writers David Walker and Frederick Douglass showed the hypocrisy of limiting that education to white men. In the middle of the nineteenth century Emerson insisted on the development of a capacity for "aversive thinking" in the service of freedom. At the end of the nineteenth century and the beginning of the twentieth, the American research university comes of age, and chapter 2 discusses pragmatism's extensions of the Emersonian vision in this context. The main figures discussed in the chapter are W. E. B. Du Bois, Jane Addams, and William James. Du Bois rejected Booker T. Washington's accommodationist vocationalism in favor of the critical capacity of liberal learning. His criticism of Washington reinforces the association of education and freedom, especially for those who have been oppressed. Chapter 3 breaks the chronological flow to discuss controversies over liberal education, from Benjamin Franklin's satire of Harvard's pretentiousness to contemporary concerns over whether a college education "is really worth it." The notion of a liberal education has long been contested in the United States, and most often the issue has been how to balance practical demands with humanistic inquiry. Calls on Harvard College to better prepare farmers were made a century before Theodore Roosevelt asked universities to instill homely virtues such as kindness, thoroughness, and thrift rather than mere intellectual skills. These complaints are echoed today by social scientists like Charles Murray and Richard Vedder, who have challenged the economic rationale for higher education. The likes of

Murray and Vedder want higher education to produce the equivalent of better farmers today. In chapter 3 we see that ambivalence about liberal learning (if not outright hostility to it) has always been intertwined with our commitments to education. In the fourth and final chapter I return to pragmatism and its commitment to lifelong learning through ongoing inquiry. John Dewey and Richard Rorty took up the cause of liberal learning precisely because it fit so well with the pragmatic ethos that linked inquiry, innovation, and self-discovery. Rejecting a view of education as narrow training, pragmatists embraced a capacious practicality that would be energized by a broad, flexible education.

The claim of this book is that broadly based, self-critical and yet pragmatic education matters today more than ever, and that it matters far beyond the borders of any university campus. The demands for useful educational results have gotten louder, and threats to liberal education are indeed profound (from government regulators, from the business sector, from within the university). In an age of seismic technological change and instantaneous information dissemination, it is more crucial than ever that we not abandon the humanistic frameworks of education in favor of narrow, technical forms of teaching intended to give quick, utilitarian results. Those results are no substitute for the practice of inquiry, critique, and experience that enhances students' ability to appreciate and understand the world around them—and to innovatively respond to it. A reflexive, pragmatic liberal education is our best hope of preparing students to shape change and not just be victims of it.

Change, some of it potentially disruptive, has come to American higher education in a very visible way in recent years. Technology promises to expand the reach of compelling teachers while significantly reducing costs. In the last couple of years, massive open online classes (MOOCs) have been prominent in debates concerning the future of higher education. Those who want to see universities become much more narrowly utilitarian embrace the classes as quick paths to the certification of marketable skills. Similarly, those who fear the further commercialization of universities see the technology of MOOCs as contributing to growing alienation and depersonalization in higher education. Although at first skeptical, I have come to believe that we can use this platform to advance liberal education. It can also be used for forms of training. No particular technology in itself enables or threatens liberal learning, but those who want to expand its range must experiment with new technologies. That's why I decided to offer a rather traditional humanities class, The Modern and the Postmodern, as a MOOC with Coursera and recruited professors from six different departments to join me in offering online versions of their undergraduate classes.

If The Modern and the Postmodern was an unlikely candidate for a MOOC, I was an equally unlikely candidate to teach one. As a university president, I don't have as much time to devote to teaching as I would like, and taking on this additional assignment, with all its unknown variables, seemed to many in my administration overly ambitious. Actually, some told me it was crazy. In addition, I was no fan of the massive online classes I'd checked out. It seemed clear to me that whatever learning happened online via lectures, quizzes, and peer-graded essays was very different from what I'd experienced in residential colleges and universities.

I was intrigued, though, by the prospect of sharing my class with a large, international group of people who wanted to study. This was really going beyond the university's campus, and I wondered if doing so would change the way I thought about teaching and learning. I certainly wasn't looking for ways to replace the campus experience, but I was open to expanding the framework within which to think about it. How *would* students learn via recorded lectures, and how would *I* know what they were learning if they were grading each other? Would there really be a "massive" number of students who wanted to take a humanities class focused on literature, history, and philosophy? Would I be able to teach effectively without the instant feedback I receive from students when I am talking with them in a classroom? And how would teaching in the online format affect the way I teach on campus and the way Wesleyan will educate the coming generations of students?

I was surprised that almost thirty thousand people enrolled in the class, but I also found the number intimidating. I was used to facing a room full of eager faces, and we usually came to enjoy one another's company as we studied together. Thirty thousand strangers I couldn't even see just scared me. My "lectures" in the campus classroom are almost totally improvised—I talk about a number of quotations from the assigned reading and respond to questions. And I say dumb things all too often, but in the classroom we always find ways to move on. In an online class, however, some silly joke I make about Freud could go viral and become my epitaph.

On our first day, the website for The Modern and the Postmodern was eerily quiet. Finally, our tech-support person discovered that we had neglected to click something akin to a "Go Live" button. We did that while I was driving my daughter home from high school. When I checked the site after dinner, I was astonished at the level of activity. Study groups were forming based on language and geography. There were Spanish and Portuguese groups, study units forming in Bulgaria and Russia and Boston and India. "Anyone in Maine?" someone plaintively inquired. (Turns out there are quite a few Courserians there.)

Geographical diversity was just the start. Some members of the class decided to begin a discussion board for older students, and many retired teachers joined in. Three couples were following the class together—all six had Ph.D. degrees—and decided to write me with questions about my definitions of the modern. Students holding down full-time jobs wrestled with Rousseau and Marx but wished the two would just "get to the point," while a graduate student in the Netherlands provided fabulous lists of secondary sources for those who wanted more reading. There were students who were in high school and dreaming of college, older folks who wanted to discuss poetry when they came home from work, and people from all over the world who just had a deep desire to continue to learn.

After about a month, we organized a Google Hangout (a visual conference call) in which several students (chosen by lottery) could participate in a free-flowing discussion about the reading and lectures. We recorded the hour-long session and made it available to everyone else in the class. One hangout included people in Calcutta, São Paulo, southwest France and . . . Rhode Island. The first question from India was about the nineteenth-century French poet Charles Baudelaire. We'd talked about his notion of the *flâneur*, the happy wanderer in the modern city. The Indian student wanted to know how I'd connect this notion to Baudelaire's interest in how our senses can be activated by powerful works of art. The student from Brazil said the week's readings, by Ralph Waldo Emerson and Ludwig Wittgenstein, were "mind blowing," and she asked how their ideas of memory related to those of the other authors we'd read.

This hour-long intense discussion wasn't a "massive" conversation; it was a colloquy mediated by technology. Thousands of other students would watch the hangout, and many of them would resume these conversations in different forms—from face-to-face meetings in cafes to virtual encounters in online chat rooms. They were eager for intellectual stimulation and cultural participation; they had a strong desire to learn how to learn—to experience great works of literature and philosophy in ways that would promote further inquiry. They had, in sum, an appetite for liberal learning that extended far beyond the college years and the campus boundaries.

Many have written about the extraordinarily high attrition rates in MOOCs. At Wesleyan we expect (almost) all of our students to complete their coursework on time, while most MOOCs have attrition rates of more than 90 percent. But saying someone "failed to complete" a free, open online class is like saying someone "failed to complete" the *New Yorker* in the week she received it. Most don't sign up for the class or the magazine for purposes of "completion." Half of those who enroll often don't even actively begin the class, while others will learn with the course rather than seek to finish it for purposes of a grade and certificate (although some do want that). There are many access points for increasing one's understanding of the world and its history. Students use MOOCs differently than students use the classroom, and we should pay attention to that rather than think the online world fails to replicate a "really real" classroom. When I teach my course on campus next year, I want to give my undergraduates the benefits of what I've learned from the online version. This will be more than just using recorded lectures as homework. It will be integrating perspectives on things great thinkers have said—and things I've said—from an amazing range of people from across the globe.

On the Discussion Forum for The Modern and the Postmodern there were any number of threads. Some commented on the teaching (happily, they were enthusiastic about the lectures), others on the grading (more than a few complaints about the peer evaluations), and still others offered complementary materials to add to our study—from songs to scholarly articles to cartoons. One student wrote about how much he enjoyed the class because it was a respite from taking care of his disabled parent. This sparked a conversation with several others who were in similar situations. Others talked of missing the excitement of being at a university, while still more talked about never having had that opportunity. At Wesleyan we embrace the label "Diversity University," but we are highly selective and admit a small percentage of the very qualified people who apply. My MOOC impressed upon me aspects of difference and inclusion I don't often encounter on my campus.

One of the threads of our discussion board asked why those in the class felt the need to keep studying. A student from Singapore wrote about our class "igniting the fire for learning," while a Swiss graduate student enrolled with his "mum" so that they would be able to discuss the material together. She'd dropped out, but he said that he finds the camaraderie online a reminder of why he went to a university in the first place. Somehow, the graduate seminars he takes in Zurich don't live up to his expectations. A student in South India related that decades after having completed formal schooling, "learning makes me feel alive." And a student who didn't say where she's from simply wrote: "Baudelaire has captured me. I love the living and the feeling and the participating in life's beauty and ugliness. I have taken to carrying *Paris Spleen* around town with me as I walk and bike."

Turns out the "massive" part of these open courses was the least interesting thing about them. My students didn't feel like a mass. It's the differences among them, and how they bridged those differences through social networks, that energized their MOOC experience and mine. Of course, like books and lectures, films and recordings, MOOCs can also be used for much more utilitarian ends, but I found in teaching one nothing necessarily antithetical to the goals of liberal education. On the contrary, the technology of MOOCs revealed that there was a wide international interest in learning for its own sake, an interest in broadening one's cultural experience and in connecting with other people who share one's passionate curiosity. My "good-enough books" class aims to combine the intertwined traditions of inquiry and cultural participation. I am trying to help my students develop their critical thinking skills while also inviting them to revere great achievements in philosophy, history, and literature. At least I want them to understand why these texts have inspired reverence as well as research. My aim, then, is to contribute to their liberal education—and this is just as true online as it is in person. Liberal learning mattered to my online students in some of the same ways it matters to my students on campus: it helps them in the process of self-discovery while bringing them into a more thoughtful conversation with the world around them.

Beyond the University is not focused on online learning or how to bend the cost curve in higher education. These are worthy subjects that have stimulated much discussion. This book steps back from current debates concerning technology and cost to argue that the calls for a more efficient, practical college education are likely to lead to the opposite: men and women who are trained for yesterday's problems and yesterday's jobs, men and women who have not reflected on their own lives in ways that allow them to tap into their capacities for innovation and for making meaning out of their experience. Throughout American history calls for practicality have really been calls for conformity—for conventional thinking. If we heed them now it will only impoverish our economic, cultural, and personal lives.

The mission of universities focused on liberal learning should be, in Rorty's words, "to incite doubt and stimulate imagination, thereby challenging the prevailing consensus."[8] Through doubt, imagination, and hard work, students "realize they can reshape themselves" and their society. Liberal education matters because by challenging the prevailing consensus it promises to be relevant to our professional, personal, and political lives. The experimentation and open-ended inquiry of a broad, pragmatic education helps us think for ourselves, take responsibility for what we do and believe, and be more aware of our desires and aspirations. This book will show that liberal education has long mattered to Americans because it increases our capacity to understand the world, contribute to it, and to reshape ourselves far beyond our years at a university.

1.

From Taking in the World to Transforming the Self

WE AMERICANS HAVE strong yet ambivalent feelings about education. We believe in its necessity, but we aren't sure how to measure its success. We know it's important for our economy and culture, but we don't trust what it does to our kids. We are as committed to learning as we are to freedom, but we are made nervous that too much learning, like too much freedom, can be a form of corruption. Every week the newspapers, magazines, and blogs are filled with stories that display the dysfunction of our K-12 educational system; we read about good schools striving to produce high scores rather than well-rounded students and about poor schools being punished for their failure to be located in affluent neighborhoods rather than helped to cope with their perilous positions in an ecology of poverty.

The discourses concerning higher education are just as conflicted, though the issues are somewhat different. Those students who manage to finish a four-year degree (even if it takes five or six years) are usually very satisfied with their college experience. Whether they go to a large public university or a small residential college, many of these students will look back with appreciation on their own intellectual and social growth during this period of their lives. Of course, there will be questions about the costs of those years. Was the investment as thoughtful as it should have been? Did the college years "pay off" enough in the long run? The numbers most frequently cited underscore that a college diploma will usually result in a significant wage premium for most people. But each family is left to wonder whether its own investment in a college education was a wise one, and as a nation we still wrestle with the question of what such an education is really for.

Of course, millions of students don't even start four-year programs, and most of those who begin two-year community colleges never earn a degree. Many students acquire more debt than they can afford, along with frustration and a sense that the system failed them. They wonder whether they should have expected to get a college education in the first place. They wonder why education matters, especially if it wasn't effective job training.

The questions raised about education in America today are not new, but they do have an urgency about them, an urgency born of the particular economic and social conditions of our time. After decades of self-confident military and economic supremacy, American official culture seems gripped by a sense of impending doom, or at least by a feeling that our children will likely have fewer opportunities than we have had. As has happened periodically throughout our history, American optimism is once again being tested.

Education depends fundamentally on our ability to generate optimism and find reasonable (defensible) ways to sustain it. When our faith in the future is shaken, whether it be by technologies we don't understand, economic competition that undermines job security, or cultural forms that challenge our sense of identity, we often criticize education as having failed to prepare us for our current predicaments. And so it has been since the Puritans first set up schools in the New World.

We start our consideration of liberal education not with the Puritans, though, but with the founding of the United States. As our democratic experiment was being launched at the end of the eighteenth century, so were debates about the importance of education. The key figure here is Thomas Jefferson, author of the Declaration of Independence and third president of the United States. Jefferson himself had an insatiable appetite for learning, and he was convinced that only by educating its citizenry could the new Republic steer a course between the hazardous rocks of governmental tyranny and popular anarchy. Jefferson was a man of the Enlightenment, and for him this meant faith that the accumulation of knowledge would improve public and private life. He was committed to a view of the United States that vested power and authority in the people (at least the free white men), and he was acutely aware that the health of the new polity was dependent on those with authority being educated in how to use it. Thus the education of the people should be the responsibility of a government elected by the people. This would create a virtuous circle of learning and a citizenry thoughtful enough to protect itself from governmental overreaching.

In the eighteenth century, there was little to support the idea that education was a governmental function. European traditions gave the church or the family the responsibility for education, and the nature of instruction much depended on the denomination with which one was affiliated. Generally speaking, the Protestant emphasis on reading the Bible for oneself demanded basic literacy, and this had had a profound impact on expanding the capacity to read to the popular classes. The New England colonies extended this movement into the political sphere by using tax dollars to pay for schooling.[1] In addition to enabling one to read the Bible, schooling was seen in political terms because an educated populace would be able to make judgments about those who wielded authority over them. Literacy was the key to acquiring information, and the ability to thoughtfully consider that information was a basic requirement of membership in the community.

The emphasis on education was not confined to the colonies in the Northeast. Although they disagreed about many important political issues, John Adams and Jefferson saw eye to eye on the necessity of education as a foundation for maintaining freedom. "Wherever a general knowledge and sensibility have prevailed among the people," Adams wrote, "arbitrary government and every kind of oppression have lessened and disappeared in proportion." Americans could be proud, he thought, of their commitment to learning: "A native of America who cannot read and write is as rare an appearance as a Jacobite or a Roman Catholic, that is, as rare as a comet or an earthquake."[2] Jefferson was similarly committed to the idea that knowledge was freedom and that literacy was the basic foundation of knowledge. Like Adams, he believed that the government could do most to protect freedom by promoting an educated citizenry.

There was, however, considerable resistance to the idea that education should be a governmental project. Insofar as one thought that education and religion should go hand in hand but also that public authorities should not promote any specific religious belief, then one would not want secular state officials interfering with schools. Education was a *moral* process, many believed, and it should not be divorced from ecclesiastic powers. Then there were those who were skeptical about the government's ability to promote education in the name of freedom and independence. Would not a government have every incentive to use publicly supported schools to indoctrinate citizens into slavish obedience?

For Jefferson and Adams, the best protection against indoctrination was more education. Only an informed citizenry would be able to see through the ruses used by governmental authorities, and exposure to the competition of ideas would allow citizens to judge who could best represent their interests. Adams, we might say, hedged his bets in this regard. Though he invested mightily in the importance of the people being able to critically evaluate information, he also supported an architecture of government that would force regular compromise among competing groups, or orders: "Orders of men, watching and balancing each other, are the only security; power must be opposed to power, and interest to interest. . . . Religion, superstition, oaths, education, laws, all give way before passions, interest and power, which can be resisted only by passions, interest and power."[3] Adams believed in education in the long run, but he wanted to be certain that checks and balances and layers of representation would prevent any particular regime from going too far too fast.

Jefferson had a more idealistic notion of an educated citizenry as the guardian of freedom. The major goal of his education proposals was "to enable every man to judge for himself what will secure or endanger his freedom."[4] The political and moral core of education was cultivating the capacity for independent judgment so as to be free from external coercion. "Man, Jefferson, believed, is most free when he is most nearly or completely self-sufficient, hence his education must be concerned with developing such inner resourcefulness."[5] All citizens should develop this capacity, and some of them would go beyond it to develop lives in which they pursued ideas for their own sake.

Jefferson's concepts of education fell into two main spheres: popular instruction of the citizenry and higher education. He introduced legislation in Virginia in 1779 to address the first issue, *On the More General Diffusion of Knowledge,* and he founded a university decades later to embody his ideas concerning the second. The legislation never passed, but its principles reverberated in American discussions of education for generations. The University of

Virginia at Charlottesville was launched with the strong imprint of its founder, and it continues to thrive today.

Jefferson's *On the More General Diffusion of Knowledge* proposed that citizens should learn the basic skills for preserving their freedom, for conducting their affairs, and for continuing to learn. Literacy and numeracy were key. It was the government's responsibility to see to this education because only if the people had such instruction could they be counted on to govern themselves. "If we think them [the people] not enlightened enough to exercise their control with a wholesome discretion, the remedy is not to take it from them, but to inform their discretion by education."[6] This was why Jefferson argued that taxpayers should foot the bill, rather than count on churches or rich benefactors to see to the people's education. Adams, who disagreed with his "frienemy" on many political questions, was of one mind with him when it came to the public's responsibility for education: "The whole people must take upon themselves the education of the whole people, and must be willing to bear the expenses of it. There should not be a district of one mile square, without a school in it, not founded by a charitable individual, but maintained at the public expense of the people themselves."[7]

Access (remember, though, just for free white males) to instruction regardless of wealth was a key component of this Jeffersonian plan. All citizens deserve a decent education. Girls would be included in elementary instruction, though he did not focus on their particular studies. But access was just the starting point. At each level, he planned to determine the most talented 10 percent of the boys, who would then be given the opportunity to continue their work at a higher level. Again, it was crucial that the state pay for those who could not afford to pay for themselves. Jefferson thought that the health of the Republic would depend on its ability to renew itself by finding talent of the first rank, and he was trying to create a system that would find gifted young men who might otherwise be overlooked because they didn't come from the right families. "The best geniuses will be raked from the rubbish annually," and the state would be able to benefit from "those talents which nature has sown as liberally among the poor as the rich but which perish without use, if not sought for and cultivated."[8]

Raking the rubbish for talent who would then be culti-vated at the public expense would prevent the creation of permanent elites based on wealth who would try to turn the government's powers to their own private advantage. Jefferson believed strongly that given the variability in human capacities and energy, there would always be elites. His notion of equality was an equality of access or opportu-nity, not an equality in which everybody wins. But he also believed strongly that without a serious effort to find and cultivate new talent, the nation's elites would harden into what he called an "unnatural aristocracy," increasingly corrupt and inept. His plan for the "diffusion of knowl-edge" aimed to create a basic level of knowledgeable citizens while providing the most talented among them with the ability to become tomorrow's elite—a "natural aristocracy," as he called it.

In Jefferson's system, those talented youngsters culled from the ranks of students in the early years of study would eventually need a strong university at which they could complete their formal education. His legislative agenda for primary education was defeated in the 1790s, however, mostly because the state representatives thought it too expensive. Jefferson continued to believe that universal primary education supported with public funds was crucial, but he could see that the antitax fervor around him made his plans politically unpalatable. So, in his later years Jefferson focused his attention on creating a new sort of university, one that embodied his particular conception of liberal learning. Jefferson had played a role at the College of William and Mary, striving to modernize the school in the wake of the American Revolution and the European Enlightenment. But he discovered how difficult university reform could be, and so he decided it would be more advantageous to start from scratch, founding a new university so that "every branch of science, useful at this day, may be taught in its highest degree." He was struggling to separate the new institution both from the influence of religious groups and from the traditions of rote traditional learning that he thought had infected Old World and New England universities. In a report of 1818, he listed the key objectives for university education: "To form statesmen, legislators and judges; to expound on principles of government; harmonize agriculture and commerce; develop reasoning facilities of our youth; And, generally to form them to habits of reflection and correct action, rendering them examples of virtue to others, and of happiness within themselves."[9] It was clear that Jefferson wanted his university to produce the leaders, the natural aristocrats, of the new nation. But what did he have in mind in saying that the school would teach branches of science "useful at this day"? And how would one determine "the highest degree"?

These were questions Jefferson had long considered. Shortly after independence, he had supported an effort to launch a national university, a project that even the hero George Washington couldn't bring to fruition. The first president had hoped that a nonsectarian university drawing on all of the states would inspire national unity. A flagship educational institution could achieve an international preeminence that would be hugely advantageous for the new nation. Benjamin Rush had laid out a plan for a Federal University in 1788, with the goal of "acquiring those branches of knowledge which increase the conveniences of life, lessen human misery, improve our country, promote population, exalt the human understanding, and establish domestic, social, and political happiness."[10] When Washington became president, he championed this idea: "A primary object of such a National Institution should be, the education of our Youth in the science of *Government*. In a republic, what species of knowledge can be equally important? And what duty, more pressing on its Legislature, than to patronize a plan for communicating it to those, who are to be the future guardians of the liberties of the Country?"[11] But Congress was not willing to ask citizens to support a university with tax dollars, and the desire for a secular institution that would foster national unity ran into opposition on the grounds of regionalism and religion. Those concerned that federal authorities would increasingly lord it over the states were never eager to see a preeminent central university. Those who thought that education without religion would lead to corruption could not countenance an institution of higher learning that did not explicitly rest upon the core principles of Christianity.[12]

Jefferson was one who supported Washington's project for a national university, and he even had the idea of importing the faculty for it from the University of Geneva. But seeing the opposition to the national plan, he would eventually focus his efforts in his own state of Virginia. In the summer of 1818 he, together with James Madison, James Monroe (then president), and a small group of other notables met in the Blue Ridge Mountains, commissioned by the state legislature to discuss their vision for publicly supported higher education. Jefferson was seventy-five years old at the time, and he took two days to travel the thirty miles from his home to the tavern in the Blue Ridge. He arrived on horseback accompanied by Madison, two aged founders of the country now trying to secure its future by establishing a public institution of higher education. Jefferson's report early on acknowledged that some felt that a university education provided merely "useless acquirements," or that this was the type of enterprise best "left to private individual effort." But he and the other commissioners at the tavern in Rockfish Gap were convinced that cultural independence and civic health required the public support of advanced work in an array of fields that were creating new knowledge. Such support would pay dividends to all because of the effective leadership that graduates would bring the state. Virginians, Jefferson noted, should not be sending their sons to Kentucky for their education, where a public institution had recently been created. Nor should the talented youth head for Europe, where they were more likely to be corrupted than educated. There should be a place of learning, an "academical village" close to home where they could fully develop their abilities. After Jefferson's skillful negotiations and imaginative presentations on the state's demography, it was determined that the university's location would be Charlottesville, just down the hill from his home in Monticello. This way he could keep an eye on things.[13]

Mr. Jefferson's university, as it came to be called, would be an engine of inquiry where the habits of study and reflection, research and conversation would lead to the betterment of students and teachers alike. "Education generates habits of application, of order, and the love of virtue; and controls, by the force of habit, any innate obliquities in our moral organization."[14] The experience of students, as he knew well, doesn't at all points stimulate the habits of moral organization that the author of the Declaration of Independence had in mind. The raucous celebrations of college men, their "inebriated insubordination," were problems in the early nineteenth century as they are in the early twenty-first.[15] But don't we still hope that our students acquire a love of virtue, even as they discover through hard work and sociability just what "love" and "virtue" might mean?

For Jefferson, the pursuit of happiness required an active mind, and engagement in the practice of open-ended research was a good in itself while often leading to positive outcomes in the world.[16] He compared the improvements brought by learning to the improvements a farmer introduced in his orchard through grafting: "Education, in like manner, engrafts a new man on the native stock, and improves what in his nature was vicious and perverse into qualities of virtue and social worth."[17]

Jefferson's university would be nondenominational. The author of the Declaration had also penned the *Notes on the State of Virginia*, a forceful articulation of the need to separate religious and political life. Religious faith was a personal matter, he argued, not based on knowledge or supported by research. One could certainly allow for private worship, but there was no point in bringing onto campus what he thought of as the idle speculations of theologians. When confronted with critics who said he was a godless corrupter of youth, he would offer Protestant churches the right to set up academies on the periphery of the school. They declined.

What would be taught at Jefferson's university? Ancient and modern languages; pure and applied mathematics; physics, botany, zoology, anatomy, and medicine; government and law; ideology, grammar, ethics, rhetorics, literature, and the fine arts. Although religion was excluded from the curriculum, it seemed little else was. Yet Jefferson consistently spoke of *useful* knowledge, or the "circle of the useful sciences."

In what ways did he think all these areas of study useful? Jefferson was a man of the Enlightenment, and for him this meant faith that the accumulation of knowledge would improve public and private life. Thus, his conception of "useful knowledge" was capacious and open-ended—and he reflected this even in his design for the campus in Charlottesville. To be sure, Jefferson's curriculum placed much less emphasis on the learning of Greek and Latin texts than many schools of the time, in favor of what he thought of as more active or modern fields. And he had a clear preference for history over literature because he found the former more conducive to moral and political instruction. Jefferson was committed to the modern: students should learn useful (not "dead"!) languages and engage in disciplines that had active research agendas. But the "sage of Monticello" was no narrow utilitarian. He himself delighted in reading classic texts in their original languages and wrote that "I feel a much greater interest in knowing what has passed two or three thousand years ago, than what is now passing. I read nothing, therefore, but of the heroes of Troy, of the wars of Lacadaemon and Athens, of Pompey and Ceasar . . . I slumber without fear, and review in my dreams the visions of antiquity."[18] Visions of the past, when tested by facts and thoughtful conversation, would develop into genuine knowledge that could be put to use in the world.

Jefferson was convinced that history, literature, and philosophy, though taught at the university, could also be studied readily enough outside of the classroom. On campus he emphasized the sciences, which along with mathematics accounted for about half of the curriculum.[19] He did this not because he believed that graduates would become scientists themselves but because the habits of mind and methods of inquiry characteristic of the modern sciences lend themselves to lifelong learning that would serve one well—whether one went on to manage a farm or pursue a professional career.[20] It is here we see the dynamic and open-ended nature of Jefferson's understanding of educational "usefulness." His approach to knowledge and experimentation kept open the possibility that any form of inquiry might prove useful.[21] This value could not be determined in advance, but, in true Enlightenment fashion, would be determined by what individuals made of their learning as they built on its practice (its "habits of application, of order, and the love of virtue") once outside the confines of the campus. The independent and free inquiry cultivated at the university would enable independent and free thinkers, citizens capable of thinking for themselves and taking responsibility for their actions in the contexts of their communities and the new Republic. That inquiry might be in grammar or zoology, anatomy or ideology—it didn't matter to Jefferson. The free pursuit of knowledge would prove useful because it helped to form free citizens beyond the university.

This leads us to one of the most important formal innovations in Mr. Jefferson's university, the freedom of students to choose their own course of study: "I am not fully informed of the practices at Harvard, but there is one from which we shall certainly vary, although it has been copied, I believe, by nearly every college and academy in the United States. That is, the holding the students all to one prescribed course of reading, and disallowing exclusive application to those branches only which are to qualify them for the particular vocations to which they are destined. We shall on the contrary, allow them uncontrolled choice in the lectures they shall choose to attend, and require elementary qualifications only, and sufficient age."[22] For Jefferson it made little sense to promise a free, open-ended education to students if they were already "destined" to pursue particular vocations, if they were forced to follow the previous generation's dictates on how they were to live their lives. Education allowed for the experience of freedom as one began to discover one's capacities, and one began to discover these capacities as they were brought into use through education. The author of the Declaration of Independence wanted students to make these discoveries for themselves, not to be told what to study because their futures had already been decided by their families, teachers, churches, or government. If the university was to be a place where one discovered and cultivated one's independence, then it made no sense to solidify it as an institution that would cement the pathways determined by the previous generation. Jefferson's university was to be a place that practiced freedom, and he hoped this would give its faculty and students a greater ability to act in accord with that freedom as republican citizens and private individuals.

Of course, it is important to remember that Jefferson's university aspired to being a place of freedom while also excluding most of the population from ever attending such a place. The University of Virginia was to be only for the most talented citizens. Those who had succeeded in the earlier levels of schooling might have an opportunity to choose their course of study, but the majority of people (women, slaves, native peoples) would never have that opportunity and were excluded from the start. Jefferson's hypocrisy regarding race and gender is legendary; his insight into structures of oppression didn't disturb his own personal tyrannies. If our unconventional third president understood that education was inexorably linked to the possibility of freedom, his conventional racism and sexism led him to think that neither women, Africans, nor native peoples should enjoy that possibility. They were not to be citizens, so they were not to be educated.

But this is already to overstate things, for there are vast differences and inconsistencies in Jefferson's views on these excluded groups. With regard to women, he admitted that "a plan of female education has never been a subject of systematic contemplation with me,"[23] yet in his 1779 plan for schooling in Virginia, girls were included through the elementary grades. Some of his contemporaries, agreeing on the importance of an educated citizenry, realized that mothers would be responsible for a good part of that instruction—and thus women, too, should have a quality education. Noah Webster and Benjamin Rush, for example, wrote on the importance of women becoming competent partners in the home and thoughtful mentors to their children in republican independence.[24] In 1819 Emma Willard argued powerfully, if unsuccessfully, for state-supported seminaries for women to be trained as professional teachers.

As a widower with three young daughters, Jefferson emphasized the importance of the girls achieving competence in domestic matters, including the ability to launch their own children in a process of learning. He urged them on in their study of foreign languages, music, science. In many respects, the education recommended for girls was similar to that for boys, but that similarity stopped well before the university.[25] There the goal was to produce leaders, and Jefferson's regard for girls and women—his understanding of equality—did not extend that far.

In regard to Native Americans, Jefferson's views were complex, not to say contradictory. He got to know many Indians as a youth, and in his travels he made sustained efforts to understand their languages and political systems. In 1785 he wrote that "I am safe in affirming that the proofs of genius given by the Indians place them on a level with whites," and he often spoke of how the political organizations of specific tribes evinced an attachment to liberty that should be emulated by the former colonists.[26] His scholarship on native peoples was consistently respectful; he used them often as examples to combat racialist degeneracy theorists popular in Europe. He spoke of a day when all living in North America would, through intermarriage, become one "continental family." But as many historians have pointed out, Jefferson the politician was a ruthless adversary to Native Americans. American Indians who got in the way of white expansion would be destroyed without mercy. And as the sage of Monticello said himself: "If we are constrained to lift the hatchet against any tribe, we will never lay it down until that tribe is exterminated."[27] Jefferson included the study of American Indian tribes in the curriculum of his new university, but he did not think there would be Indians studying there.

As Jefferson's published views on Native Americans have to be seen in relation to his policies concerning westward expansion of the new country, his views of Africans must be seen in the context of his personal and political connection to the institution of slavery. Jefferson was a slaveholder who also hated the institution because he thought it degraded everyone who came in contact with it: "There must doubtless be an unhappy influence on the manners of our people produced by the existence of slavery among us. The whole commerce between master and slave is a perpetual exercise of the most boisterous passions, the most unremitting despotism on the one part, and degrading submissions on the other. Our children see this, and learn to imitate it; for man is an imitative animal. This quality is the germ of all education in him."[28] Jefferson complained of "boisterous passions," yet fathered several children with his slaves, most famously with Sally Hemmings, the half sister of his wife. There is a sea of literature now trying to understand these contradictions (or condemn them), but here our interest is their relation to his views on education. In *Notes on the State of Virginia*, Jefferson called for an end to slavery while also presenting his views on the natural intellectual inferiority of blacks. Jefferson repeats some of the racist appraisals of Africans by white writers of his time. He recycles the standard calumnies about their work ethic and about the natural ugliness of their hair and skin. Perhaps most important, from his perspective, was his conclusion that blacks were capable of very little learning: "Comparing them by their faculties of memory, reason, and imagination, it appears to me, that in memory they are equal to the whites; in reason much inferior." As he famously added, although they might be gifted in music, "misery is often the parent of the most affecting touches in poetry.—Among the blacks is misery enough, God knows, but no poetry."[29]

For Jefferson, Africans could not proceed in the journey of enlightenment, and so they could not become full citizens. In 1780, as governor of Virginia, he wrote that they should not continue to be made slaves, but neither could they live among the free (and educable) citizens of the United States. Jefferson was not thinking just about the limited future of blacks as he tried to imagine a postemancipation society; he was worried about the permanent prejudices of the ex-masters, and the ex-slaves' inability to forget the massive injustices done to them—"ten thousand recollections, by the blacks, of the injuries they have sustained."[30] How could black and white Americans ever learn, ever truly engage in mutual education, given the horrible history in which they were entangled? "Indeed I tremble for my country when I reflect that God is just: that his justice cannot sleep for ever: that considering numbers, nature and natural means only, a revolution of the wheel of fortune, an exchange of situation, is among possible events: that it may become probable by supernatural inter-ference! The Almighty has no attribute which can take side with us in such a contest."[31] The governor-slaveholder goes on to express hope that things are beginning to get better, that "the spirit of the master is abating, that of the slave rising from the dust" in ways that would avoid a violent reversal of oppressive roles.[32] The author of the Declaration imagines, even strongly desires, that the black slaves will be free. But he cannot imagine them living side by side in equality with whites, and so he offers a scheme that would send the millions of blacks to a new colony: "For if a slave can have a country in this world, it must be any other in preference to that in which he is born to live and labour for another."[33]

Here we seem to have come upon the limits of Jefferson's views of education, the point at which his creed that learn-ing in the broadest sense sets you free runs aground on his prejudices that some people just can't learn how to learn. Jefferson could not imagine African poetry, could not abide the possibility of stirring narratives written by an ex-slave, but African Americans themselves would extend the Jeffersonian faith in education as the path toward freedom.

Here we will look at just two powerful examples. The first is David Walker's 1829 *Appeal to the Coloured Citizens of the World*. Walker, whose father was a slave and mother a free black, grew up in North Carolina and eventually settled in Boston. He was a fervent evangelical, a shopkeeper, and active in the local Freemasonry organization. Walker wrote for abolitionist newspapers and was committed to inspiring blacks to seize the freedom that was rightfully theirs, rather than appeal to whites to grant it to them as a gift. Walker writes a call to arms for enslaved blacks, urging them toward an intellectual and spiritual independence that would empower them to overthrow the tyranny of their masters. Just a few years after Jefferson's death, Walker explicitly attacks both the founder's comments on the inferiority of blacks in *Notes on the State of Virginia* and the wrongs of slavery more generally. Walker doesn't want a slaveholder deciding that slavery is an evil; he wants the slaves themselves to articulate this judgment and then take the appropriate actions. "For my own part, I am glad Mr. Jefferson has advanced his positions for your sake; for you will either have to contradict or confirm him by your own actions, and not by what our friends have said or done for us; for those things are other men's labours, and do not satisfy the Americans, who are waiting for us to prove to them ourselves, that we are MEN, before they will be willing to admit the fact."[34] Walker asks, "How to prove that we are MEN?" And he answers in what had become the classic Enlightenment (not to say Jeffersonian) formulation. We will show that we are men by showing that we can learn. Education is the path to freedom:

> I pray that the Lord may undeceive my ignorant brethren, and permit them to throw away pretensions, and seek after the substance of learning. I would crawl on my hands and knees through mud and mire, to the feet of a learned man, where I would sit and humbly supplicate him to instill into me, that which neither devils nor tyrants could remove, only with my life—for colored people to acquire learning in this country, makes tyrants quake and tremble on their sandy foundation.
>
> The bare name of educating the coloured people, scares our cruel oppressors almost to death. But if they do not have enough to be frightened for yet, it will be, because they can always keep us ignorant, and because God approbates their cruelties, with which they have been for centuries murdering us. The whites shall have enough of the blacks, yet, as true as God sits on his throne in Heaven. (37)

Walker closes his *Appeal* by using the author of the Declaration to attack the author of *Notes on the State of Virginia*. Hear your own words, he calls: "Compare your own language ... extracted from your Declaration of Independence, with your cruelties and murders inflicted by your cruel and unmerciful fathers and yourselves on our fathers and on us" (80). To be sure, the religious rhetoric throughout the *Appeal* is not Jeffersonian, but the faith in education surely is. By "seeking after the substance of learning," from Walker's perspective, oppressed blacks will prove that they are human; they will realize (actualize) their own humanity. In so doing, they will "scare their cruel oppressors" and set themselves free.

Walker's *Appeal* certainly did frighten the white establishment. His powerful call for justice and insurrection was printed in three editions in 1829 and immediately created a backlash. The pamphlet circulated through black societies, churches, and businesses. It was said that Walker sewed copies into the used clothing he sold in his store. In the South, blacks were arrested, or far worse, if they were suspected of having copies of the text, and a bounty was put on the author's head. The state of Georgia was willing to grant $10,000 to anybody who could hand him over alive, and $1,000 to anyone who would murder him.[35] The pamphlet's message, linking education, freedom, and justice, continued to reverberate as radical abolitionism began to develop in the 1830s, though Walker himself died a year after its publication, probably of tuberculosis.

The second example of an African American writer seizing on a Jeffersonian commitment to education as freedom comes from Frederick Douglass's autobiography. Douglass's book was published after he had already become a well-known figure in abolitionist circles as an extraordinary speaker and a gifted debater. He relates how as a boy he was sent to live with the Auld family in Baltimore, and that most of his time as a child was spent under the supervision of the pious Sophia. Sophia spent much her time reading the Bible or singing verses from it, and for the little Frederick this "awakened my curiosity in respect to this *mystery* of reading and roused in me the desire to learn." The little slave boy made rapid progress, and his mistress wanted to show him off to her husband. Auld's reaction was decisive, and deeply formative for Douglass: "Learning will spoil the best nigger in the world. If he learns to read the Bible it will forever unfit him to be a slave. He should know nothing but the will of his master, and learn to obey it. As to himself, learning will do him no good, but a great deal of harm."[36] This "new and special revelation" was a turning point for Douglass, as he puts it, the "first anti-slavery speech" that made a difference to him. " 'Very well,' thought I. 'Knowledge unfits a child to be a slave.' I instinctively assented to the proposition, and from that moment I understood the direct pathway from slavery to freedom" (97). The direct pathway to freedom is education, and education is based in literacy because once you can read you have the independence to learn on your own.

This is a Jeffersonian moment in Douglass's life, and in American history, even if Jefferson himself never imagined that men like Douglass would ever experience such moments. The fact that America paid tribute to liberty and equality while brutally enslaving millions outraged Douglass, and that kind of outrage helped fuel the abolitionist movement in the decades preceding the Civil War. Jefferson's blindness and hypocrisy aroused the scorn of abolitionists, for they knew that the principles of freedom could not be indefinitely applied to only a limited class of people. For Douglass, these principles were tied to education, as he experienced it in the arc of his own life. In a powerful 1852 speech denouncing America's celebrations of the Fourth of July, Douglass pointed out that all could see that slaves were people because they could be educated. Indeed, there were laws against teaching slaves to read because their educability was testimony to their rights to equality and freedom: "It is admitted in the fact that Southern statute books are covered with enactments, forbidding, under severe fines and penalties, the teaching of the slave to read and write. When you can point to any such laws in reference to the beasts of the field, then I may consent to argue the manhood of the slave."[37] As a young slave, Douglass had experienced the epiphany of education—that by learning to learn he was already acquiring freedom. State legislatures in the South recognized this as well and through vicious subjugation were determined to prevent education from spreading. Frederick Douglass and David Walker, like John Adams and Thomas Jefferson in the previous generation, understood that education, learning to learn, would spread, unless ferocious violence was used to stop it.

Jefferson inherited and transformed Enlightenment legacies as he helped to launch the American experiment. The patterns he wove combining education, freedom, and responsible citizenry remain essential to the fabric of our culture. In the Jeffersonian design, government assumes responsibility for the education of its citizens, so that, in turn, citizens could intelligently take responsibility for their government. Jefferson was inspired to reimagine the modern university, seeing it as a place where students could have the experience of liberal learning, learning for its own sake, with confidence that their education would be useful in the broadest and deepest sense — not just on campus. For Jefferson, faculty at the institution should be active scholars, not drill masters. They should model the creed of education as freedom — not just repeat the catechism. Free inquiry by its very nature would not slide members of the campus community into preordained slots, for it would create new questions as it answered old ones. The questions formulated on campus would lead far beyond the university as lifelong learning shaped the culture of the Republic and its citizens. We shall see in a later chapter that Jefferson's devotion to education as freedom struck some as insufficiently practical, others as insufficiently spiritual. Critics wanted either a more directly utilitarian training or a stricter regime of religious observance. But not long after his death, Jefferson's devotion to education as freedom became an inspiration to those who wanted to extend his vision of Enlightenment even as they found his racism abhorrent. That inspiration has helped reignite a commitment to liberal education generation upon generation.

Ralph Waldo Emerson was born while Thomas Jefferson was president. Emerson's father was a Unitarian minister in Massachusetts, a path that he himself would follow after his graduation from Harvard College. But the ministry didn't suit Emerson. After his young wife, Ellen Tucker, died of tuberculosis, he found himself increasingly alienated from the formal dimensions of religious life. He sought something more direct, something at once more personal and more universal. "I have sometimes thought that in order to be a good minister," he wrote, "it was necessary to leave the ministry."[38] The "corpse-cold" routines of religious observance got in the way of an experience of God and the world—of God *in* the world, as Emerson would come to think of it. Emerson would dedicate his working life to writing and lecturing, always trying to find a way to convey his sense of experience so as to provoke his readers and auditors to open themselves to a deeper acknowledgment of their own lives. The opening to experience would be an opening toward education, toward personal and social progress.

The concepts of "experience" and "progress" had been central to Jefferson and his contemporaries. John Locke had made experience the core of his understanding of the self and of knowledge. Since he thought of the individual as a blank slate, it was experience that actually created the self—the recording and recollection of the outside world came to *be* the self. From the Lockeian perspective, things experienced were in the outside world, and it was through their impact that the self was formed. Locke was providing an alternative to René Descartes' picture of the mind as generating its own ideas and intuitions. Jefferson was indebted to this Lockeian tradition, and his approach to education made diffusing knowledge very much like sharing experience. If we could accumulate, critically evaluate, and share the patterns of experience that occurred throughout society, we would create the conditions for progress.

Emerson transforms the Enlightenment notion of experience that was so crucial for Jefferson. Although he maintains an emphasis on the encounter with the outside world, the theater of that encounter is shifted to consciousness. That is, Emerson is focused on how we take the world in, and on how our intuitions, in collaboration with the world, generate new ways of thinking and feeling. Rather than the mind being the slate upon which the world leaves impressions, he conceives of it as an active partner with the world. Education, then, will not just be the diffusion of knowledge gathered from inquiry and experiments. Education will include an increased awareness of, even the cultivation of, the self. The point of education, for Emerson, will not just be the accumulation of knowledge or even the building of character. The point will be the transformation of the self and of one's culture.

Emerson had a powerful influence on intellectual life in the mid-nineteenth century, as he toured the country lecturing on topics as varied as nature, compensation, wealth, and "the Over-Soul." Having left the pulpit, he discovered a much more effective way of preaching on spiritual and philosophical topics; his essays and poetry reached elite culture as well as the literate public. He was a force to be reckoned with, and the great writers of the day, from

Whitman to Poe, from Hawthorne to Thoreau, tried to come to terms with his teaching. As Harold Bloom has said, Emerson "is the theologian of the American religion of self-reliance," and his influence (whether acknowledged or not) has remained powerful for 150 years.[39]

Emerson's two texts that most powerfully articulate his beliefs about the power of learning to create independence are "The American Scholar" (1837) and "Self-Reliance" (1841). The first was an address given on Phi Beta Kappa Day at Harvard College. The occasion was highly charged. Emerson's father and brother had delivered speeches marking this day in years past, and each had been greeted warmly by the Unitarian establishment. But Emerson had already broken with these elites, and his friends among the transcendentalists expected him to support their view that everything worth knowing came through self-knowledge. Emerson's friends had no use for Calvinist ideas of predestination, and they rejected the notion that one could prove religious truths through empirical research. The Harvard-Unitarian elites, on the other hand, saw transcendentalism as "the new heresy," and Emerson was ready to substantiate their antagonism by directly criticizing their desire for power, money, and admiration. He "was going to Harvard to have a duel."[40]

Emerson began his address with some gentle irony. The occasion for his talk, the "holiday" of Phi Beta Kappa Day, marked the importance of literature and study for the Harvard community. As such, the special day at the university was "simply a friendly sign of the survival of the love of letters amongst a people too busy to give to letters any more. As such it is precious as the sign of an indestructible instinct." Emerson is doing two things here as he begins to teach. He is noting the poverty of the (commercially oriented) present, too busy "to give to letters," and he is counting on a natural instinct that could be cultivated so as to reinvigorate our ability to so give—to nurture and contribute to culture. He knows that American civilization is viewed as "busy," as being constituted by what he calls "the exertions of mechanical skill."[41] The time is ripe for a change, for no longer should the enterprising young Republic simply be turning to the Old World for its cultural nourishment.

Emerson's diagnosis of the situation is grave, for our long dependence has deformed us; it has turned us into anything but real human beings: "The state of society is one in which the members have suffered amputation from the trunk, and strut about so many walking monsters,—a good finger, a neck, a stomach, an elbow, but never a man." "Man is thus," he writes, "metamorphosed into a thing, into many things" (46). The situation is dire, but that is why the time is ripe. Emerson will announce the end of this "long apprenticeship" again and again, as he tries to find ways for events and actions to "sing themselves" through him (45).

There are three main forces that shape the scholar: nature, the past, and action. Nature is chaotic, confronting mind with energetic turbulence. As thinking develops, the confusion of nature recedes and the mind comprehends patterns and shapes in the world around it. As the "Thinking Man" matures, he begins to see that "nature is the opposite of the soul, answering to it part for part. . . . The ancient precept 'Know thyself,' and the modern precept, 'Study nature,' become at last one maxim" (48). The second main influence on the scholar is the mind of the past, and that comes through to the present in books, objects, and institutions. But for Emerson it is crucial that this influence not be one characterized by the passivity of the scholar. Real readers are "active souls" who use the past in order to focus their own powers. This is in contrast to the "bookworms" he sees being produced by schools and colleges. These institutions cultivate passivity and are content to show the scholar examples of great work as if to say, "This is good . . . let us hold by this" (50). By contrast, Emerson sees education as finding ways to allow the past to push us forward. We must, he insists, be inventors to read well. He readily admits that guidance from the best books is a great service, but this service can turn into corruption if it teaches subservience to the material—if it teaches dependence. Higher education should ignite students' spirit and intelligence with the materials from nature and the past, not merely show them how to digest these materials. "Colleges, in like manner, have their indispensable office—to teach elements. But they can only highly serve us, when they aim not to drill, but to create; when they gather from far every ray of various genius to their hospitable halls, and, by the concentrated fires, set the hearts of their youth on flame" (51–52). Emerson here is radicalizing the notions of university education that Jefferson developed when founding the University of Virginia. The enemy for the founding father was rote learning; the plague was to be trained for a destiny that had already been chosen for you. Emerson builds on Jefferson in calling for institutions of advanced learning to inspire and transform through creativity.

The third influence on the scholar should be action. Emerson's vision of the thinking man is muscular; he envisions the individual out in the fields, not just taking in the world but reacting to it, shaping it. "The so-called 'practical men' sneer at speculative men, as if, because they speculate or *see*, they could do nothing." "Action," Emerson writes, "is with the scholar subordinate, but it is essential. Without it, he is not yet man. Without it, thought can never ripen into truth." The scholar welcomes labor because it enhances vitality and can feed thinking. He must, as in all things, be careful not to take on work just because others think it important. His work, his action, must emerge from his independence and vitality: "Instantly we know whose words are loaded with life, and whose not" (52).

In his address, Emerson calls for an active scholar, open to inspiration from nature and from the past, an inventive laborer and creative reader, because he wants this person to have a formative role in our culture. Education teaches one not to follow the crowd but to discover one's own way: notice everything yet imitate nothing. The independent, educated person is able to "resist the vulgar prosperity that retrogrades ever to barbarism" (56). In the nineteenth century, as today, it was crucial to resist the view of education as merely job training but also to emphasize that true education must go beyond the campus. By resisting the vulgar striving for prosperity that Emerson sees around him in the young Republic, scholars find their independence, their freedom. "The world is his who can see through its pretension" (57).

Emerson's call for independence is neither a call for (scholarly) detachment nor for educated sophistication. One of the most remarkable things about this extraordinary speech is the plea near its end to pay attention to the everyday, to the ordinary. His scholars are not raising their sights from the hoi polloi to some ethereal world of art and leisure. No, in being "the world's eye" the new American scholars will pay attention to everything around them. "The literature of the poor, the feelings of the child, the philosophy of the street, the meaning of household life, are the topics of the time. . . . I ask not for the great, the remote, the romantic . . . I embrace the common, I explore and sit at the feet of the familiar, the low. Give me insight into today, and you may have the antique and future worlds" (61). Jefferson moved away from what he regarded as the European university's concentration on the venerable to a focus on the modern—to those areas of inquiry where knowledge is being created. Emerson is here going beyond that shift, accentuating its democratic potential. He is announcing a new view of the scholar, a new view of how one can continue one's education throughout one's life. Scholars are those who take up into themselves the capacities of their time, the contributions of the past, the hopes of the future. They are the university of active knowledge (62). Today we might say that through that active knowledge they design the future.

Emerson's Phi Beta Kappa address is meant to shake the audience, to rouse it from its dogmatic slumbers, from its subservience to European models of education. "We have listened too long to the courtly muses of Europe," he announces, but it doesn't have to be this way (62). Education can create a "nation of men," not mere appendages, to recall the image with which he began his talk. Education can create people who know how to walk on their own feet, who experience the dignity of labor and the freedom to speak their own minds: new, active scholars for a new, active nation.

Emerson's call for a new scholar, not a mere bookworm but "Man thinking," was pointedly addressed to a Cambridge audience at America's oldest college. Harvard had recently gone through an administrative shake-up and was retreating from progressive currents in American culture at the time. Its new president, Josiah Quincy, was put in place for his managerial capacities, not for his intellectual leadership, and the Board of Trustees was much taken with the *Yale Report* of 1828, which had called for a greater reliance on the classics (more on that in the next chapter). In other words, Harvard seemed to be following Yale in mounting a rearguard action against modern educational ideas. For Quincy, "an essential part of education was proper dress and social associations . . . he intended his students to be 'high-minded, high-principled, well-taught, well-conducted, well-bred gentlemen' . . . like himself, perfect members of Boston's commercial class."[42] Rather than being an incubator of creativity or a gateway to more robust experience, Harvard appeared to many to be a crucible of conformity, or simply a "private refuge for the wealthy."[43] Harvard's emphasis on wealth would result in increasingly intellectual narrowness, which would in turn lead to an even greater emphasis on wealth. Emerson saw real learning as transformational, and the narrow paths for success marked out by the university's elites made such an education all but impossible.[44] The goal of transformational teaching should not be merely the diffusion of knowledge or the advancement of science but the development of a more capacious self with a greater ability to experience the world and creatively respond to it.

Emerson returned to the themes of "The American Scholar" many times throughout his writings and lectures, but for our purposes the essay "Self-Reliance" offers the most significant elaboration of his idea of how education, "thinking man," and freedom are interrelated. After an epigraph in verse, "Self-Reliance" begins with the words "I read the other day," and the whole essay considers how we can take in elements of the world (through reading and other forms of experience) without merely mirroring what we absorb. Emerson wants us to "stand on our own two feet," but he does not want us to stand in isolation or ignorance. "I read the other day," he writes, "some verses written by an eminent painter which were original and not conventional."[45] They seemed to Emerson verses of "latent conviction," and that is why he responds to them: "In every work of genius we recognize our own rejected thoughts: they come back to us with a certain alienated majesty" (129). We don't want to mimic the work of genius; from Emerson's perspective, we want to put ourselves in a position to recognize some portion of ourselves in the work's majesty. To do so is to learn to respect one's own capacities and not just to appreciate external greatness: "There is a time in every man's education when he arrives at the conviction that envy is ignorance; that imitation is suicide; that he must take himself for better, for worse, as his portion; that though the wide universe is full of good, no kernel of nourishing corn can come to him but through his toil bestowed on that plot of ground which is given to him to till." Education is key; Emerson knows we need instruction. But we will never learn who we are and how we are related to the rest of the world unless we reject education as imitation and have faith in "our own portion." "Trust thyself," he writes, "every heart vibrates to that iron string" (130). "Self-Reliance" explores how one can trust oneself, walk on one's own two feet, without walking alone. How one can accept "the society of your contemporaries" without becoming dependent on them, accept the events in the world without becoming a slave to them. Negotiating these tensions for Emerson is the core of one's education.

The opposite of self-reliance for Emerson is conformity, and there are several warnings in the essay about its dangers. Conformity is the enemy because it is so pervasive; how difficult it is to find your self when you are chasing the approval of others! And the pleasures of imitation are seductive and subtle — even the nonconformist may just be imitating a model of rebellion. This is something one has seen in university settings for a very long time. But not only there. The hermit who thinks he is protecting his integrity by going off to the woods, whether it be Emerson's friend Thoreau or some back-to-the-land undergraduate, may still be following some chimera of virtue in solitude. "It is easy in the world to live after the world's opinion; it is easy in solitude to live after our own; but the great man is he who in the midst of the crowd keeps with perfect sweetness the independence of solitude" (134).

Preserving in "perfect sweetness the independence of solitude" without giving up the genuine experience of society — of friendship, of learning, of joint endeavor — this is the goal of self-reliance. How is education relevant to this goal? In a very general sense, one must learn not to be corrupted by the voices of society, which are "in conspiracy against the manhood of every one of its members." "Whoso would be a man must be a nonconformist" (132). But conformity can come in many guises, for there are many parties or sects to which one can adhere. Where's the harm in learning of these alternatives and joining in? "This conformity makes them not false in a few particulars, authors of a few lies," Emerson writes, "but false in all particulars. Their every truth is not quite true" (134).

In addition to the pressure to conform that comes from society, Emerson also emphasizes the pressure that comes from the effort we often make to be consistent with ourselves. "The other terror that scares us from self-trust is our consistency," he writes (135). People come to have expectations of us, and we are loathe to disappoint them. Thus, he distinguishes his "trust yourself" from a desire to be the same person over long stretches of time: "A foolish consistency is the hobgoblin of little minds. . . . With consistency a great soul has simply nothing to do" (136). The self of tomorrow may not *be* the self of yesterday, and so the thing one should trust is not some stable entity but an openness to experience. The Enlightenment view of the self that comes from Locke had already stressed that the self was not a divine, unchanging substance but instead the product of sensation and memory. Emerson is a critic of the tyranny of memory, of the effort to be true to your past. "But why should you keep your head over your shoulder? Why drag about this corpse of your memory, lest you contradict somewhat you have stated in this or that public place? Suppose you should contradict yourself; what then? It seems to be a rule of wisdom never to rely on your memory alone, scarcely even in acts of pure memory, but to bring the past for judgment into the thousand-eyed present, and live ever in a new day" (135). To live ever in a new day means escaping the tyranny of the past. "Man is timid and apologetic; he is no longer upright; he dares not say 'I think,' 'I am,' but quotes some saint or sage. He is ashamed before the blade of grass or the blowing rose. These roses under my window make no reference to former roses or to better ones; they are for what they are; they exist with God to-day. There is no time to them. There is simply the rose; it is perfect in every moment of its existence" (141).

Like books for the active reader in "The American Scholar," in "Self-Reliance" history is to be engaged for inspiration or instigation, not to be mined for imitation. Emerson playfully evokes Descartes' "I think therefore I am" in the passage just quoted, but he does so to situate his own argument, not to borrow the authority of a deceased philosopher. "Your genuine action will explain itself and will explain your other genuine actions. Your conformity explains nothing" (137). In any case, Emerson would add, we shouldn't be wasting time in explanation; we should have the courage to trust ourselves.

But how can one have education without some imitation of others and without some consistency from those who are doing the learning? Great teachers don't want to create clones, but much of the power of their pedagogy comes from their example—their embodiment of learning. Strong students are not rote learners, but they must have the capacity for disciplined study and for absorption of the material they are trying to make their own. Teachers and students alike may seem to lose themselves in their subjects, but they can emerge more themselves through the learning process. They emerge more self-reliant.

Emerson's message in "Self-Reliance" is that we become more at home in the world as we learn to stand on our own feet. "Discontent," he writes, "is the want of self-reliance; it is infirmity of will." By insisting on ourselves, by refusing imitation and conformity, we reject useless regret and idle criticism. "Regret calamities, if you can thereby help the sufferer; if not, attend your own work, and already the evil begins to be repaired" (147). Attend to your own work—that's a core message of Emerson's essay. When you do your own work, you begin to repair the world without trying to conform to it. There are many distractions that reduce our ability to find which work is our own. Toward the end of his essay, Emerson singles out property and the institutions that protect it as powerfully corrosive forces undermining self-reliance. He knows well the American affection for material goods; he knows how "busy" his compatriots are in commerce. But like Jean-Jacques Rousseau, he recognizes that we disperse ourselves in our possessions, and we become ever more vulnerable as we acquire more things that require protection. Attending to our own work doesn't mean accumulating stuff. It means finding for ourselves work it feels we were meant to do.

Education should offer us the opportunity to discover the kinds of work we find meaningful. This is very much connected to Jefferson's synthesis of education and freedom. Jefferson saw education as a path away from the tyranny of custom and government. Earlier generations should not dictate the choices of the young. Students would benefit from the diffusion of knowledge to find the kind of learning and the kind of work for which they were most suited. Enlightenment education would provide independence to young Americans in their new country. Learning would help set them free from the past. Emerson built on this Jeffersonian legacy in underscoring the dangers of conformity that arose even as one spread knowledge. Freedom of inquiry and discussion were not enough; they had to be accompanied by a turning of the self away from imitation and conformity. Education had the double duty of diffusing new knowledge while also teaching the kind of aversive thinking that might just undermine the authority of those who were spreading the Enlightenment word in the first place. Emerson was acutely aware of the paradoxes of his position to "prate of self-reliance" (142). He wanted no imitators in his call to avoid imitation.

This kind of paradox has remained key to liberal learning in America. Our universities are supposed to have the authority and creativity to conduct research, produce knowledge, and spread it to as many people as possible. Jefferson thought this would increase the freedom of students as they became active citizens. But our universities are also supposed to be places that protect critical thinking—thinking that undermines belief in received wisdom. Engaged learners are anticonformists aiming to discover more about who they are and what kind of work they might find most meaningful—not simply to accept what has been handed to them, even by the most reputable scholars. The productive tension between the university as a bastion of productive research and the campus as a place for aversive thinking and personal transformation has been at the heart of liberal education since the nineteenth century. This is a tension bequeathed to us from the thinkers we have studied in this chapter. We should not try to resolve it, or wish it away through an effort to reduce learning to the certification of narrowly vocational skills. The tensions embodied in American higher education have helped make this sector one of the most dynamic facets of our country's cultural life. These tensions and the forms they have taken over the last hundred years are the subjects of our next chapters.

2.
Pragmatism

From Autonomy to Recognition

JEFFERSON AND EMERSON set high ideals for liberal education in America. Learning prepared one for autonomy and for citizenship. Learning also led one away from the crowd; it helped one escape mere imitation and opened access to authenticity. Finally, education was meant to offer us the opportunity to discover the kinds of work we would find meaningful. For both Jefferson and Emerson, however, these arguments about education were mostly relevant to upper- and (perhaps) middle-class students. How relevant is it to talk about "finding meaningful work" when available work might necessarily involve drudgery and worse? How relevant is it to talk of citizenship and aversive thinking to students who first and foremost are desperate to escape from poverty? These questions became increasingly pertinent toward the end of the century, and with particular acuity for African slaves and their descendants. The same questions, alas, are still asked today.

In 1903, Booker T. Washington, the most influential black public figure in the United States, voiced the following complaint: "There were young men educated in foreign tongues, but few in carpentry or in mechanical or architectural drawing. Many were trained in Latin, but few as engineers and blacksmiths. Too many were taken from the farm and educated, but educated in everything but farming."[1] Washington was a passionate advocate for an intensely practical education for ex-slaves and their descendants. He was born a slave on a small farm in Virginia and after the Civil War found work in the mines of West Virginia. After his education at the Hampton Institute, Washington was convinced that only by achieving economic success would blacks ever be recognized by white Americans as full members of society. Education should make people self-reliant, to be sure, but for Washington self-reliance was first and foremost the ability to earn a decent living.

The Hampton Institute in Virginia made a decisive impact on Washington. When he arrived there at age sixteen, the mission of the school had already been firmly established by its founder, Brigadier General Samuel Armstrong: "The thing to be done was clear: to train selected Negro youth who should go out and teach and lead their people first by example, by getting land and homes; to give them not a dollar that they could earn for themselves; to teach respect for labor, to replace stupid drudgery with skilled hands, and in this way to build up an industrial system for the sake not only of self-support and intelligent labor, but also for the sake of character."[2] Intelligent labor would create moral uplift because one would take responsibility for one's labor and take care of one's own portion. Independence of mind and spirit would be derived from economic independence.

The Hampton Institute began as a refuge and basic educational center for ex-slaves and quickly became a potent force in educating hundreds of black teachers who would in turn educate thousands of children. Students would learn to work with their hands as well, and it was on this combination of basic academics and training in a trade that Washington built his illustrious career as an educator, institution builder, and public figure. After working at Hampton as a teacher and administrator, he was sent to create a like institution in Alabama. He helped launch the Tuskegee Institute in 1881 with a mission to teach the basic trades and the core academic skills necessary for teachers.

Washington was not just a teacher at Tuskegee; he was its chief fund-raiser and institution builder. He appealed to blacks who were looking for a path out of economic impoverishment, and he appealed to whites who appreciated his decision not to demand political or cultural change. Washington was an "accommodationist," willing to work within the structures of legal subordination of blacks in the South as long as he was able to promote black economic advancement. Rather than demand the enforcement of the right to vote, he asked for help in training tradesmen and teachers. Rather than demand social equality, he appealed to those who were interested in having a more educated workforce. His message resonated with wealthy industrialists, high-toned educators, and even presidents.

He was the most famous black man in America, and he was considered by many in both the South and the North a fine representative of his race.

But as the nineteenth century was coming to a close, Washington also had critics who complained that his accommodationist approach doomed blacks to second-class status. They argued that full citizenship, not just economic advancement through a trade, was essential, and that a broad, liberal education prepared the independence of mind essential for real citizens. Foremost among these critics was W. E. B. Du Bois. Born in Great Barrington, Massachusetts, shortly after the end of the Civil War, Du Bois came into his own when Washington was at the height of his fame. The younger man was a prodigious intellectual with a slew of degrees—bachelor diplomas from Fisk and Harvard, a Ph.D. from Harvard (he was the first black person to receive one there), with continued graduate work in Berlin. He was a classics professor and a historian who wrote sociology (highly praised by Max Weber), poetry, plays, and fiction—to name just some of the genres in which he worked.

In his magisterial *The Souls of Black Folk*, Du Bois was careful to acknowledge the important work that Washington had accomplished in setting up the Tuskegee Institute and training tradesmen. But Du Bois was biting in his criticism of Washington's acceptance of social and political subservience, which went hand in hand with the denigration of a broad, liberal education for blacks. The South, Du Bois emphasized, feared educated blacks: "And the South was not wholly wrong; for education among all kinds of men always has had, and always will have, an element of danger and revolution, of dissatisfaction and discontent. Nevertheless, men strive to know."[3] Men strive to know just as they strive for freedom, as Frederick Douglass had emphasized, and educational institutions should aim to stimulate that hunger for knowledge—not just contain it within their walls.

Whereas Washington recognized the American desire for material success and wanted to build progress for African Americans on their ability to be successful in the economy, Du Bois emphasized political and civic equality, along with the education of youth according to ability. This is not the place to examine the dispute between these black leaders in any detail, except to emphasize how Du Bois draws on the Jeffersonian-Emersonian traditions of freedom and self-reliance while promoting a broad, liberal education. For education was at the core of the differences between these leaders. Du Bois rejected what he saw as his rival's anti-intellectualism. "The pushing of mere abstract knowledge into the head means little," Washington had written. "We want more than the mere performance of mental gymnastics. Our knowledge must be harnessed to the things of real life."[4] Du Bois didn't disagree, but he wanted to broaden what might count as "the things of real life" so that the pursuit of happiness wouldn't be reduced to the pursuit of dollars. "The function of the university is not simply to teach bread-winning, or to furnish teachers for the public schools, or to be a centre of polite society; it is, above all, to be the organ of that fine adjustment between real life and the growing knowledge of life, an adjustment which forms the secret of civilization" (47).

Du Bois was acutely aware that the "fine adjustment" between life and knowledge was especially problematic in a society of oppressive racial inequality, a society that even after emancipation had denied many blacks the most rudimentary education. He was committed to the ideal that education was a path to freedom, but he also acknowledged the fact that different people need different kinds of educational opportunity. "If these things are so, how foolish to ask what is the best education for one or seven or sixty million souls! shall we teach them trades, or train them in liberal arts? Neither and both: teach the workers to work and the thinkers to think; make carpenters of carpenters, and philosophers of philosophers, and fops of fools. Nor can we pause here. We are training not isolated men but a living group of men,—nay, a group within a group. And the final product of our training must be neither a psychologist nor a brickmason, but a man" (48).

Education is for human development, human freedom, not the molding of an individual into a being who can perform a particular task. That would be slavery. The descendants of slaves needed to be taught, and in the decades just after the Civil War thousands of black teachers graduated from colleges and spread out across the South. To focus all black education on trades and commerce in the early years of the twentieth century made little sense to Du Bois: "If white people need colleges to furnish teachers, ministers, lawyers, and doctors, do black people need nothing of the sort?" (58)

Given his own experience, Du Bois would countenance no ceiling upon the education open to blacks. But this did not mean that he expected thousands would follow his lead to Harvard and Berlin to study classics, history, and philosophy. This is why he, like Jefferson in the early days of the Republic, emphasized "the education of youth *according to ability*." Some would learn to read and write before going on to trades or agricultural work; others would display the talent and drive to deepen their education and make their own contributions to knowledge. Du Bois referred to this latter group as "the Talented Tenth," leaders of the race whose example would instill pride and inspire others to go beyond what had been declared to be their limitations. Members of the Talented Tenth would be able to compete with anybody as long as they were given the basic equality that made competition viable in the first place. But Du Bois was less interested in the elite's ability to compete in the white world than he was in its capacity to "guide the Mass away from the contamination and death of the Worst, in their own and other races."[5] The Talented Tenth should receive a broad college education so as not to mistake economic advantages for cultural progress: "All men cannot go to college but some men must; every isolated group or nation must have its yeast, must have for the talented few centers of training where men are not so mystified and befuddled by the hard and necessary toil of earning a living, as to have no aims higher than their bellies, and no God greater than Gold."[6] The elite should participate in the ongoing transmission and creation of knowledge, enabling them to remind others that there is more to life than the almighty Dollar.

Drawing on an Emersonian notion of aversive thinking, Du Bois' conception of a black elite has had a powerful impact on the "double-consciousness" of African American public intellectuals for over a hundred years.[7] Du Bois was a brave and incisive critic of American racism, and he had faith, as did Frederick Douglass, that education was key to the struggle against that racism. But Du Bois did not want education merely to make blacks more like successful whites, if that meant pursuing monetary gain without consideration of a deeper knowledge of the world and of one's fellows. "If we make money the object of man-training, we shall develop money-makers but not necessarily men; if we make technical skill the object of education, we may possess artisans but not, in nature, men. Men we shall have only as we make manhood the object of the work of the schools—intelligence, broad sympathy, knowledge of the world that was and is, and of the relation of men to it—this is the curriculum of that Higher Education which must underlie true life. On this foundation we may build bread winning, skill of hand and quickness of brain, with never a fear lest the child and man mistake the means of living for the object of life."[8]

The Emersonian rhetoric here is striking, and in the period of aggressive industrialization and the glamorization of wealth it was more important than ever to critique those who confused the "means of living for the object of life." Du Bois didn't want his Talented Tenth to pursue the equivalent of what today might be internships at Goldman Sachs or aspire to join the cool folks in the Hamptons or Malibu. Successful conformity to white America would lead only to the perversion of their talents. "It is industrialism drunk with its vision of success," Du Bois wrote in words that ring true still today, "to imagine that its own work can be accomplished without providing for the training of broadly cultured men and women to teach its own teachers, and to teach the teachers of the public schools."[9]

"Broadly cultured men and women" were men and women who had access to higher education. The university would open worlds of knowledge to its students, and it would be a haven for the creation of new knowledge for those who made their careers there. Like Emerson, Du Bois expected that an authentic education might put one at odds with the spirit of industrialization and commerce that increasingly defined American culture. But unlike Emerson, Du Bois expected his educated elite to have a responsibility to guide people, even to save them. "Education must not simply teach work—it must teach Life. The Talented Tenth of the Negro race must be made leaders of thought and missionaries of culture among their people. No others can do this work and Negro colleges must train men for it. The Negro race, like all other races, is going to be saved by its exceptional men."[10]

If higher education gave one access to a kind of freedom, it also bestowed an awesome responsibility. Universities, in Du Bois' view, not only created self-reliant scholars, they produced missionaries of culture who should aim to save their brothers and sisters.

While Du Bois was a student at Fisk, Harvard, and Berlin, universities were going through massive changes. Fisk University, founded in Nashville to educate ex-slaves, was only about twenty years old in 1885 when Du Bois began his undergraduate study there at age sixteen. He had been sent to Fisk by the city fathers of Great Barrington, a small town in western Massachusetts in which there were only a few dozen black families. The young man's talents were recognized by the local leaders, and after he was orphaned, they arranged for him to head south to continue his education. Academically, Du Bois was very prepared, but he was shocked to discover the reality of African American culture and of white oppression in the South. He took various jobs to make ends meet, and while teaching in the countryside he became more aware of the violent suppression of black rights that followed the end of Reconstruction. The violence of white supremacy may not have been taught in the school's classrooms, but Du Bois would never forget it. The vibrancy of the culture of the ex-slaves was also part of the undergraduate experience at Fisk, and the contrast with his own New England origins was striking. This, too, he would always remember.

Du Bois graduated in three years and then made his way back to Massachusetts, to Harvard University, where he would begin by completing another undergraduate degree. Harvard, though more than two centuries old, had recently taken radical steps to reinvent itself. A prime mover in these changes was Charles William Eliot, who became president of the school in 1869. At that time his alma mater was still focused on building the character of and putting a polish on the sons of America's commercial and professional elite. But that was about to change. Over the course of his presidency, Eliot established the modern research university in Cambridge. Gone was the emphasis on helping children become adults through requirements and strong mentors. Instead, a system of electives led students to advanced seminars followed by the possibility of professional training. Research, not character building, was king.[11]

Harvard was hardly on the cutting edge of innovation, but under Eliot's leadership it liberalized the undergraduate curriculum and developed highly structured professional and advanced degrees. This gave rise to a significant rift in the Ivy League, with Princeton's president James McCosh as Eliot's chief antagonist at the end of the nineteenth century. Princeton believed its undergraduates should have their studies directed through much of their first two years. A liberal education meant exposure to certain traditions of learning, and only after participating in these traditions would a student be allowed to make his own way. Harvard under Eliot stood for the freedom of the elective system: if the students were smart enough and mature enough to be admitted, he argued, then they should be able to develop their own intellectual itinerary. In this regard he was moving closer to Jefferson's founding vision for the University of Virginia. Apart from a required writing course, undergraduates were left to follow or develop their passions—rather than pursuing a vocation or acquiring a specific set of useful skills. In college one pursues "the enthusiastic study of subjects for the love of them without any ulterior objects."[12]

For Du Bois this seemed an ideal learning environment, and in Cambridge he followed his passion for studying philosophy. As he notes in his autobiography, he was bountifully served. He became friends with William James, who had a decisive impact on his thinking. Josiah Royce was a mentor, and he soaked up Kant's *Critique* "in the upper rooms," reading with George Santayana. He excelled in his studies and stayed away from the white undergraduates. He was there to learn the best of what a university had to teach, and perhaps in Nashville he had already learned the lessons he needed about young white men. Du Bois was celebrated by the college community when he completed his B.A. at Harvard, and he gave a stirring address at commencement. One might say he was living the dream, but it would be more accurate to see him as a man on a mission.

The next stage in the mission was to attain the highest certification of intellectual achievement there was: the academic doctorate. This form of certification had been given a great boost by Eliot's reforms. If the undergraduate years were to be laced with freedom, postgraduate education had to be rigorously structured and demonstrably linked to achievement in research or capacity to practice a profession. In the past, Harvard students had simply chosen to attend medical school or law school instead of pursuing an undergraduate degree. It was only in the last decades of the century that the bachelor's degree became a prerequisite for professional study, and the Ph.D. (which now one could pursue only after earning a B.A.) became the standard certification of worthiness to teach college students. This meant there would be a professionalization of the university faculty, with authorization to guide graduate work becoming the highest level of attainment. More traditional colleges, with their emphasis on the building of character among undergraduates, saw themselves being eclipsed by the research university, with its emphasis on the training of experts.

This new model of a research university was a powerful import from Germany. The German seminar was a hothouse of research-based learning, and American universities were eager to hire its products. In the wake of the Napoleonic period, German universities had been reformed to serve neither the state nor the church. Universities would serve *Wissenschaft*, scientific knowledge, and this meant that they had to be bastions of free inquiry. The institutions were not there for the sake of the students or to facilitate learning. They were not there to produce leaders for the nation or citizens who could act responsibly. The mission of the modern university was to create new knowledge, and it did so by promoting research. We will return to this mission and its tensions with liberal learning later in this book.

The German research university model was imported to the United States to institute reforms at some of this country's oldest schools and it helped launch some of the newer ones. The Johns Hopkins University opened its doors in 1876 (without any place for undergraduates) with

a German-trained faculty to bring research-based serious-
ness to American shores. No character building here—one
expected publishable results! Other schools followed suit.
Du Bois, who wanted to connect his training in philosophy
with a historical approach to the race problem, knew that
study in Germany would expand his intellectual horizons
and his marketability as an academic. He set his sights on
the University of Berlin, from which the German influence on international scholarship emanated with force.
Having no money, he appealed to former president
Rutherford B. Hayes who, as head of the Slater Fund, had
complained that he couldn't find a black man worthy of a
scholarship to Europe. Though Du Bois was at first turned
down, his strong persistence resulted in a grant and a loan
to continue his studies in the crucible of the new social
science, Berlin.

Living outside the United States gave Du Bois a very
different perspective on his country: "[In Germany] I
found myself on the outside of the American world, looking in. With me were white folk—students, acquaintances,
teachers—who viewed the scene with me. They did not
always pause to regard me as a curiosity, or something sub-
human; I was just a man of the somewhat privileged student rank."[13] His interests turned to political economy, and
the historical study of politics and industrialization were
his primary fields of study. German social science was taking off, and his professors convinced him that dramatic
social reform and policy renewal could emerge from rigorous social science research. Such reforms had happened

in Germany in the decade or so before he arrived, instituting the beginnings of the social welfare state. The University of Berlin was not just training research specialists; from this young American's perspective it was preparing intellectuals to make positive, even radical, contributions to reshaping their societies.[14] "If I had not gone to Germany," Du Bois recalled years later, "I would have been locked in a completely colored world, Self-sufficient and provincial."[15] Many American universities were adopting German paradigms of research in political science, history, and what would soon become the new field of sociology. American academics were impressed by their rigorous methods and strong empirical findings. Du Bois, for his part, found in German social science a model of engaged scholarship that he would use to take on the racist structures against which he had vowed to struggle.

Although he pursued specialized graduate training, throughout his long career, Du Bois repeatedly defended liberal education against those who saw it as impractical. In an address at the Hampton Institute in the beginning of the century, he lamented that "there is an insistence on the practical in a manner and tone that would make Socrates an idiot and Jesus Christ a crank."[16] At one of the centers of industrial learning for blacks, Du Bois argued that its doctrine of education was fundamentally false because it was so seriously limited. What mattered in education was not so much the curriculum on campus but an understanding that the aim of education went far beyond the university. And here is where Du Bois issued his challenge: "The aim of the higher training of the college is the development of power, the training of a self whose balanced assertion will mean as much as possible for the great ends of civilization. The aim of technical training on the other hand is to enable the student to master the present methods of earning a living in some particular way. . . . We must give our youth a training designed above all to make them men of power, of thought, of trained and cultivated taste; men who know whither civilization is tending and what it means."[17]

Du Bois recognized that not everyone could be educated in this way, although here he says that this is because of economic considerations, not because of the varying abilities of students. But he is clear: "The ideal would be to train every man in this way, and toward that ideal we tend."[18] Du Bois held on to the core values of a liberal education, having experienced very different models at Fisk, Harvard, and Berlin. He understood well the attractions of the specialized research university, but he was devoted to the capacity-building dimensions, the power-enhancing dimensions, of liberal learning. In his own writings, he showed himself fully capable of playing the role of the expert, of the social scientist expanding the boundaries of knowledge. But expertise depended upon a foundation of liberal learning rather than being a substitute for it. For Du Bois, as for Jefferson and Emerson, there were powerful links between a broad education and self-assertion, between self-reliance and freedom. But Du Bois added a deep social connection to their emphasis on individual freedom. Technical competence was not to be disparaged, but neither should it be allowed to overshadow the form of education through which citizens discovered their humanity and their power to act on it.

As an African American child growing up in the Berkshires, or even as a naive young college student in Tennessee, Du Bois would have been a most unlikely candidate for reinvigorating the ideals of liberal education. But in addition to growing up black in post-Reconstruction America, in addition to resisting the overarching maw of industrialization in this country's most triumphalist industrial period, Du Bois reached intellectual maturity at a time when the winds of reform were picking up in American cities, and when pragmatism was coming into its own at American universities. In Jane Addams these two tendencies came together in a commitment both intellectual and political, and it is to her example we now turn.

Like Du Bois, Jane Addams grew up in the shadow of the Civil War. Her father John was one of the founders of the Illinois State Republican Party, and she came of age worshiping the legacy of Lincoln. As a young girl she dreamed of going to Smith College, a bastion of liberal learning for women, which she hoped might launch her toward a career in medicine. Her father had other ideas and insisted she attend the Rockford Seminary for girls. She certainly thrived in her years at Rockford, but the school aimed to train missionaries, and Addams had already decided that this was not to be her path. She was determined to continue her education at Smith and then practice a socially useful profession. She worked hard at the seminary, getting first-rate grades and fully participating in the intellectual life of the institution. But whatever her intellectual gifts, her father was firm about the appropriate pathway for girls. Upon her graduation in 1881, he regretted that she had worked so hard in her educational pursuits and decided that she should settle down to more familial, more feminine, concerns.

But her father died that summer of an acute appendicitis, and suddenly Jane was adrift on the turbulent seas of freedom, responsibility, and uncertainty. She had a young relative to care for, but now she also had financial independence. Her father was no longer blocking her from continuing her studies, but she seemed unable to move forward. Frozen among the alternatives before her and suddenly unsure of her way, she grew increasingly distraught. In 1882 she collapsed and was diagnosed with a nervous disorder. The remedy prescribed by the eminent neurologist S. Weir Mitchell was as simple as it was brutal: lots of rest, no physical or intellectual stimulation, and a moral prescription to stop being so selfish. The cure would be to conform to dominant cultural models, and the pressure to take that cure was enormous.[19]

But Jane Addams's mind proved stronger than the conformist cultural forces arrayed against it. She continued her education, though not at Smith College. Instead, she traveled in Europe, taking to the road to study music, art, and history. A very privileged mode of learning, to be sure, although Jane's material wealth never allowed her to escape from a crippling depression. Somehow along the way she discovered her life's work: helping the poor while really listening to them. This combined the self-sacrifice that psychiatry and Christianity were demanding of late nineteenth-century women with a public project that spoke to her intellectual and social ambitions. She emerged from depression through work for others.[20] The result was the founding of Hull House in 1889, a "settlement" in which educated women would live among poor (and often immigrant) families, providing them with educational and cultural opportunities. Addams would always emphasize that she worked *with* her coresidents and that she learned from them as they did from her. They were building a community together. Her model was mutuality and cooperation, a form of nonresistance that drew on the Christianity that she had rediscovered in her reading of Tolstoy. These ideas also allowed her to avoid the path of narrow self-assertion and ambition, much as her neurologist had recommended in the years of her illness.

Whether or not one calls the work of Hull House ambitious, it certainly had a powerful impact on the country: "Nearly every piece of major reform in the years 1895–1930 comes with Jane Addams's name attached in one way or another."[21] Addams became for some time the most beloved woman in America, though as a pacifist during WWI she was labeled "the most dangerous woman in America" by Teddy Roosevelt and hounded as a subversive. The Nobel Peace Prize was one of the countless awards offered to recognize her work locally, nationally, and internationally.

Two of Addams's concepts are particularly pertinent to
the development of American ideas of liberal learning. The
first is the "snare of preparation," a notion that sprang from
an experience she described in *Twenty Years at Hull House*
(1910). She relates that when confronted with the horror of
poverty in East London she distracted herself with an intellectual detour. Avoiding the suffering just in front of her,
she found herself thinking instead of writer Thomas De
Quincey's inability to issue a warning to a couple he saw in
immediate danger until he recalled the exact words of a
warning Achilles spoke in the *Iliad*. Instead of reacting to
the grave situation before her eyes, Addams was thinking of
De Quincey's initial failure to react to the situation before
his eyes. Education had bred avoidance; knowing the *Iliad*,
knowing De Quincey, had become impediments to action.
Were we "lumbering our minds with literature" instead of
reacting to the "vital situation spread before our eyes"?
Addams became convinced "that the contemporary education of young women had developed too exclusively the
power of acquiring knowledge and of merely receiving impressions; that somewhere in the process of 'being educated' they had lost that simple and almost automatic
response to the human appeal, that old healthful reaction
resulting in activity from the mere presence of suffering or
of helplessness; that they are so sheltered and pampered
they have no chance even to make 'the great refusal.' "[22]

This was, as we might say today, a "high-class problem."
Addams was certainly broadening her education by traipsing
around Europe, and she had the financial independence to

do so. But she realized (after being fascinated by a bullfight, "studying it" without feeling) that her education was no longer a preparation for life; it had become a substitute for living. "It is easy to become the dupe of deferred purpose," she wrote in retrospect. This realization led her to continue her education by working in the community—rather than fixing to get ready to do so. We might note that contemporary liberal arts education often tries to defeat deferred purpose by blending traditional on-campus study with opportunities to work off campus. Whether one calls this service learning, civic engagement, or community partnerships, it all can be seen as a response to what Addams, like Tolstoy, had recognized as the "snare of preparation"—educated inertia.

Another one of Addams's ideas that remains key to rethinking an effective liberal education is "affectionate interpretation." She employs the term in "The Modern Lear," a speech she delivered reflecting on the Pullman strike of 1894. The strike was a milestone in American labor relations on many levels, but for Addams the events marked the bloody transition away from a paternalistic industrial system in which owners were mini-sovereigns who were supposed to know what was best for their companies (and employees). The original strikers lived in Pullman, Illinois, a town set up by the owner of the company to meet all the needs of his workers, with those needs (and the prices workers must pay) determined solely by the head of the company. In the wake of the economic crisis of the early 1890s, Pullman cut wages and increased living expenses in "his" town. Striking workers were able to initiate a broad boycott of railroads around the country, but eventually the federal government intervened to break the strike and jail the union's leaders.

Addams saw in these events the tragic failure of people from different groups to understand one another—particularly the failure of paternalistic leaders to understand those whom they thought they were entitled to lead. "[Pullman] cultivated the great and noble impulses of the benefactor, until the power of attaining a simple human relationship with his employees, that of frank equality with them, was gone from him. . . . He and his employees had no mutual interest in a common cause. . . . Was not the grotesque situation of the royal father and the philanthropic employer to perform so many good deeds that they lost the power of recognizing good in beneficiaries? Were not both so absorbed in carrying out a personal plan of improvement that they failed to catch the great moral lesson which their times offered them?"[23]

The great moral lesson for Addams was that the age of the ethic of "individual striving" was over, and that the new generation coming of age in the early twentieth century must instead build an ethic on "mutual relationships and responsibilities."[24]

Addams clearly aligned herself with the labor movement in her speech when she said matter-of-factly that "we are all practically agreed that the social passion of the age is directed toward the emancipation of the wage-worker." But she just as clearly made an argument that "class conflict" was not a sufficiently "generous" concept for understanding the kind of social progress that the country required. She wanted to create alliances across class lines, and she firmly believed in an ethical imperative to "look all men in the face, as if a community of interest lay between."[25] Many of her progressive friends (and generations of social theorists) thought her naive in this regard, even reactionary. Appalled by the vicious tactics used by the government and by companies to defend wealth, many had sympathy for what seemed the necessarily violent tactics of those who were demanding their fair share. Addams was well aware of these critical perspectives, but she insisted on the possibility of acknowledgment across difference. Justice, she insisted, would come through an ability to recognize the legitimacy of other points of view, other vital interests. Social progress would become possible through "affectionate interpretation."

Affectionate interpretation is the imaginative effort to see things from the point of view of others, and this is especially important when faced with major differences. It is much too easy to mount a critique of positions whose weaknesses we detect. It is more challenging and more rewarding to try to comprehend why what looks to us as a weakness might in fact make a great deal of sense from another's point of view. Education, from Addams's perspective, must not merely make us more adept at defending ourselves against those with different agendas. Education should increase our powers of empathy and our ability to act in concert with others: "The cultivated person is the one who uses his social faculties, his interpretative power, the one who . . . put[s himself] into the minds and experiences of other people."[26]

Addams's thoughtful rejection of "self-assertion" in politics, ethics, and education is a powerful contribution to the emergent American tradition of liberal education. Like Du Bois', her work serves to leaven the emphasis on individual autonomy and intellectual self-reliance with the ingredients of social responsibility and civic engagement. These ingredients depended on compassion and fidelity to move beyond individualism. Du Bois reminded his educated elite, his Talented Tenth, of their responsibility for the "uplift" of the race. He expected that the power of education would stay connected with solidarity of social purpose. Addams also saw education as linked to social purpose, and the link for her came through the cultivation of fellow feeling. Education should result not in the snare of preparation, but in a turning of the individual toward public engagement in support of social progress. From her perspective, we learn through the connections we forge with others. Without the imaginative effort to acknowledge the contrasts with people different from ourselves, we fall into intellectual and moral stagnation. Through this effort, we may discover what we might have in common with people who seemed quite different from us.[27] This is why diversity has been ever more important for institutions that aim to foster liberal learning.[28] A liberal education should continually confront us with the perspicuous divergences that strengthen our ability to understand differences from various perspectives even as we learn to understand commonalities. The engaged, empathic pragmatism developed by Du Bois and Addams has been a deep resource for American educators for the last hundred years.

Pragmatism was America's great contribution to philosophy at the beginning of the twentieth century, and we've already encountered one of its key figures, William James, in our discussion of Du Bois. James had an important impact on Du Bois' early intellectual development, and it may have been his professor's push to see thinking in the thickness of reality that helped Du Bois move away from more esoteric pursuits to grapple with the problems of politics, history, economics, and race.[29] James was never Addams's teacher, but he was a great fan of her work. When she borrowed the philosopher's phrase "the moral equivalent of war" to describe the passion she hoped to incite on behalf of social reform, James was delighted. It is "hard to express the good [the book] has done me," he wrote her, "in offering new points and annihilating old ones."[30]

James was older than both Du Bois and Addams, having been born almost twenty years before the start of the Civil War. His own education was idiosyncratic, as he moved with his family to Geneva, London, and then back to America before returning to Europe for new courses of study. Emerson was James's godfather, and the young man seemed to embody the seer of Concord's advice to be guided by whim rather than consistency. William had strong interest in the sciences, except when he was seized by the impulse to study painting or to travel. As Louis Menand nicely put it, James held " 'that every gush of feeling should be followed by adequate action.' And he was a person who had many gushes."[31] After studying painting James went to Harvard Medical School but then left to join a zoological expedition on the Amazon. He returned to complete medical school, but he never did practice medicine. Instead, he eventually became an instructor at Harvard in comparative physiology before creating there the first psychology laboratory in the United States in the mid-1870s. But James would joke that he was never one for sustained lab work. He stayed at Harvard but became a professor of philosophy, the field in which he made some of his most original contributions.

James was not, alas, just happily following whim from one field to another. He was often racked by doubt, and he struggled with debilitating depression. His intellectual appetite, his curiosity about ideas, people, and action survived his psychological difficulties, and in the end he understood that the stimulation of appetite—rather than finishing a meal—was what made life interesting. In the spring of 1870 he read the French philosopher Charles Renouvier, and this proved decisive for his subsequent intellectual development and thinking about education. James began to leave behind the quest for certainty that had characterized philosophy, instead focusing on thinking as a way of coping with reality. We shouldn't try to squeeze our aspirations into a framework of logical perfection, he recognized; we should consider what we are getting out of our efforts. After reading Renouvier, James focused on the ways that our beliefs and actions help shape the universe rather than more or less accurately correspond to it.[32] The rejection of certainty and the emphasis on the active agency of human beings carries over to James's thinking about liberal education. The point of learning is not to arrive at truths that somehow match up with reality. The point of learning is to acquire better ways of coping with the world, better ways for the world as it is.

In 1899 William James published *Talks to Teachers on Psychology: And to Students on Some of Life's Ideals*. The second of the talks to students is called "On a Certain Blindness in Human Beings."[33] He begins the lecture by reminding his listeners that our judgments about things depend on the sensations the things arouse in us. It's other people's feelings that we have a hard time perceiving, although we often make judgments about them nonetheless. The blindness to which James refers in his title is our inability to see the values and meaning that other people attribute to their experience of the world (including their experience of us). Our feelings about our own duties and actions are our "vital secrets." We are external to one another: "Hence the stupidity and injustice of our opinions, so far as they deal with the significance of alien lives. Hence the falsity of our judgments, so far as they presume to decide in an absolute way on the value of other persons' conditions or ideals." "The meanings are there for others, but they are not there for us." "The spectator's judgment is sure to miss the root of the matter, and to possess no truth" (630).

James tells of his own wandering in the hills of North Carolina and his perception of the blight the settlers had brought to the land.

> The forest had been destroyed; and what had "improved" it out of existence was hideous, a sort of ulcer, without a single element of artificial grace to make up for the loss of Nature's beauty.... Talk about going back to nature! I said to myself, oppressed by the dreariness, as I drove by.... No modern person ought to be willing to live a day in such a state of rudimentariness and denudation.
>
> Then I said to the mountaineer who was driving me, "What sort of people are they who have to make these new clearings?" "All of us," he replied; "why, we ain't happy here unless we are getting one of those coves under cultivation." I instantly felt that I had been losing the whole inward significance of the situation. Because to me the clearings spoke of naught but denudation, I thought that to those whose sturdy arms and obedient axes had made them they could tell no other story.... I had been as blind to the particular ideality of their conditions as they certainly would also have been to the ideality of mine, had they had a peep at my strange indoor academic ways of life at Cambridge. (631)

James talked to students about how people are often blind to one another, enclosed within their own worlds of experience, and capable only of (mis)translating the experiences of others into their own terms. He saw a recognition of this blindness as "the basis of all our tolerance, social, religious, political. The forgetting of it lies at the root of every stupid and sanguinary mistake that rulers over subject peoples make" (645).

In his talk to students, James does not discuss how he came to acknowledge his own blindness, how he came to recognize how much he was missing. But he does provide some hints. Most of the lecture after his North Carolina story is taken up by long quotations from writers describing the inward significance of something that we might otherwise never see. We learn through the vivid description of points of view that would have otherwise remained hidden to us. Literature, not argument, helps us to overcome, or at least recognize, our blindness. Robert Louis Stevenson tells the story of teenage boys concealing a light beneath their jackets as they roamed across a town. Nobody could see the lanterns, but the pleasure in knowing one had such a concealed light was all the greater for its hiddenness. Observers would be completely deceived if they looked at these lads, Stevenson notes, because "the poetry runs underground" (633). James quotes the writer's approach to understanding experience: "The true realism, always and everywhere, is that of the poets: to find out where joy resides, and give it a voice far beyond singing" (634). James turns to Wordsworth and to Whitman, but also to his philosophy colleague Josiah Royce and to travelers' accounts of their encounters with nature. In all cases he notes the limits of instrumentalism, emphasizing that in our hurry to find the point of an activity, we may indeed miss that which can infuse the activity with broader meaning. He is well aware of the American penchant to discover the "bottom line" of a pursuit—what concrete thing did we get out of doing *that*? After all, James's pragmatism was itself often associated with a narrow instrumentalism, and the philosopher himself had talked about the "cash value" of an idea. Perhaps it's to break such associations that he celebrates Whitman's meanderings in New York, the poet's celebrated "loafing": "From the deepest point of view, who knows the more of truth, and who knows the less,— Whitman on his omnibus-top, full of the inner joy with which the spectacle inspires him, or you, full of the disdain which the futility of his occupation excites?" Overcoming a certain blindness means overcoming our judgment of another's apparently futile occupations. It means being open to the experience of joy, open to experiences like Whitman's "satisfied attention" with the "mere spectacle of the world's presence" (640).

Although James notes that there is no recipe for achieving this openness, teachers are in a privileged position to help us recognize the ways in which we all fail to see, pay attention to, and connect with the experiences of others. The different examples he gives in the lecture of the "underground poetry" of daily life or encounters with nature are meant to remind his audience of ways that we might come to see significance in things to which we had hitherto been blind. Teachers can help students become more aware of the different levels of meaning that might be found within the same situation when examined from different perspectives. Teachers, in other words, don't just impart skills for specific tasks; they also guide students to think allegorically and to puzzle out the diverse ways through which people give significance to their lives. "Education, enlarging as it does our horizon and perspective," James wrote, "is a means of multiplying our ideals, of bringing new ones into view"(657). This is one of the core aspects of liberal education. The blindness of which James spoke is always a danger in teaching, leading to solipsism and to dogmatism rather than to the kind of aversive thinking so prized by Emerson and James. As teachers, we find ourselves (or should I say we *can* find ourselves) in a position to call attention to this blindness, to show how it works and whom it serves: "If we cannot gain much positive insight into one another, cannot we at least use our sense of our own blindness to make us more cautious in going over the dark places? Cannot we escape some of those hideous ancestral intolerances and cruelties, and positive reversals of the truth?" (646)

After long quotations from writers extolling the meaning they find in pursuits that don't appear useful from the outside, James offers a commandment by way of conclusion: "It absolutely forbids us to be forward in pronouncing on the meaninglessness of forms of existence other than our own; and it commands us to tolerate, respect, and indulge those whom we see harmlessly interested and happy in their own ways, however unintelligible these may be to us. Hands off: neither the whole of truth nor the whole of good is revealed to any single observer" (644–45).

James's broad understanding of learning as overcoming blindness to other points of view was crucial to Du Bois, Addams, and the emerging tradition of liberal education in America. For Du Bois and Addams, education was a path of empowerment. Learning to become an autonomous human being, Du Bois emphasized, was going beyond learning a trade. It meant exercising the freedom to participate in whatever realm of society and politics one chose. For Addams, education was also linked to freedom and participation, ideals for which women were engaged in active struggle during her entire lifetime. She found that engaged learning, learning in community, provided a path to freedom through service and collaboration. Seeing another person's point of view from the inside was much easier when you worked side by side with that person.

James emphasized that looking for the "whole inward significance" of another's situation is a crucial dimension of any inquiry that takes us beyond the comfortable borders of our own insular groups. Teaching is neither preaching to the choir nor energizing a base of believers. In crossing borders, we don't only confront strangers when we teach; we also find people who desire acknowledgment and mutual recognition. In so doing, we can teach our students to become teachers of themselves and others well beyond their university years. This path to lifelong learning is a cornerstone of American liberal education. Learning to become citizens eager to understand those around us as we understand ourselves is also a cornerstone of American

democracy. Although this is not the only kind of understanding that can be produced in the classroom, it is a crucial one in a culture that recognizes the value of engaged
diversity—that recognizes that we all get a vote in the
evolving constitution of our universe.

3.
Controversies and Critics

∎

SO FAR WE have explored the deep roots that the tradition of liberal education has in American soil, and we have seen that efforts to nurture these roots have been intertwined with articulations of freedom, self-reliance, progress, and truth. Along with this cultivation of liberal learning there has been persistent criticism of our educational institutions' paltry cultural and societal harvests. In this chapter we turn to critics of liberal learning and examine their complaints about the meager fruits of higher education.

The most illustrious self-taught American from the founding period is surely Benjamin Franklin. Artisan, inventor, businessman, and philosopher, Franklin was a walking advertisement for the new type of person who would develop in the North American colonies. His formal schooling ending when he was a child, Franklin apprenticed with his printer brother James in Boston. James had started an independent newspaper, the *New England Courant*, and the combination of printing and publication turned out to offer Ben just about the perfect on-the-job training. But like many an intern in our own time, Ben wanted to do more than just learn the trade from the bottom rung of the ladder. When big brother rebuffed his efforts to write for the newspaper, he submitted letters for publication under a pseudonym (Mrs. Silence Dogood). These attracted considerable attention — more, apparently, than an anonymous trainee should. Franklin couldn't continue to conceal his authorship, and so at seventeen fled his apprenticeship, heading to Philadelphia to make a new life for himself.

One of Franklin's "Mrs. Silence Dogood" letters lampoons Harvard College, that "famous Seminary of learning." He explains how parents consult their purses, not their children's abilities, when deciding whether their offspring should make their way to the college: at the gates of learning, it's really money that counts. Franklin satirizes the idleness of the students and the uselessness of much of what is offered for study. He is particularly harsh on theology, but it seems he had little use for most of what passed for higher education in his day: "I reflected in my Mind on the extream Folly of those Parents, who, blind to their Childrens Dulness, and insensible of the Solidity of their Skulls, because they think their Purses can afford it, will needs send them to the Temple of Learning, where, for want of a suitable Genius, they learn little more than how to carry themselves handsomely, and enter a Room genteely, (which might as well be acquir'd at a Dancing-School,) and from whence they return, after Abundance of Trouble and Charge, as great Blockheads as ever, only more proud and self-conceited."[1]

This complaint about America's elite colleges—that they produce pride and conceit, not practical knowledge—will find echoes from Franklin's time until our own.

Franklin, though, was by no means an anti-intellectual. A man of limitless curiosity, he constantly sought to expand his own thinking and capacity for experiencing the world. He was an inventor and was proud to describe himself as living in the Age of Experiments. Franklin was also intensely social, and he looked to his relations with others to help in his perpetual project of self-improvement, what today we might call lifelong learning. In his *Autobiography* he describes a group he organized for weekly discussions of topics of mutual interest:

> In the autumn of the preceding year [1727], I had form'd most of my ingenious acquaintance into a club of mutual improvement, which we called the Junto; we met on Friday evenings. The rules that I drew up required that every member, in his turn, should produce one or more queries on any point of Morals, Politics, or Natural Philosophy, to be discuss'd by the company; and once in three months produce and read an essay of his own writing, on any subject he pleased. Our debates were to be under the direction of a president, and to be conducted in the sincere spirit of inquiry after truth, without fondness for dispute or desire of victory; and to prevent warmth, all expressions of positiveness in opinions, or direct contradiction, were after some time made

contraband, and prohibited under small pecuniary penalties.[2]

The Junto met in various configurations for over forty years. Under Franklin's guidance, it gave rise to the American Philosophical Society in 1743, whose mission was to "spread useful knowledge in the colonies." The organization continues to this day.

Why was Franklin so critical of Harvard College yet so dedicated to these less formal educational vehicles? Two reasons stand out. For Franklin, Harvard reeked of wealth and hierarchy, elements that undermined learning because they inhibited experimentation. It wasn't that wealth itself was evil for Franklin; he was a great friend of businessmen and thought that political life had much in common with markets. But wealth that led to inherited privilege was an evil in Franklin's eyes, and an institution of higher education would be pernicious insofar as it cemented unearned advantage, blocking the way for the energetic and ambitious. He also saw that colleges were hierarchical because learning was directed by professors whose authority often exceeded their knowledge. Franklin had developed an aversion to the paternalistic apprenticeship system in which seniority trumped industry and ability, and such a system was replicated in academic institutions. The Junto, by contrast, was built on fraternal or associative bonds. Like a republic, it depended on a ground of equality. Apprentices viewed their masters as holding them back from making their own way in the world, whereas a republican system would thrive through mutual encouragement.[3] Mutual instruction, learning from one's peers, inspired a sense that effort, not privileges and wealth, would determine one's lot.[4] Insofar as colleges reinforced the notion that one's role in life had been fully cast, Franklin thought them vastly inferior to mutual instruction through his eighteenth-century version of social networking.

After his success with the Junto group and his development of a lending library to support independent inquiry, Franklin proposed an academy that would be run neither by the government nor by the church—a "distinctively American academy."[5] A good Enlightenment man, he took his bearings from Locke, though Franklin's approach was more republican and much less beholden to the traditions of classics or religion than was Locke's. As historian Merle Curti pointed out long ago, Franklin's education existed to enhance the middle-class man's ability to achieve success in politics and in commerce—and this would come at the expense of the aristocrats, who would no longer be able to monopolize social or political power.[6] Franklin would have no truck with a university that tried to put a noble veneer on middle-class strivings. Knowledge was power, and that was nothing to be ashamed of. One didn't need a university to teach one how "to enter a room genteely." Franklin was focused on the practical; an educated person should have a better chance of changing the world.

Franklin's Academy would develop into the first independent, non–religiously affiliated college in the colonies. Although the curriculum would emphasize history, especially insofar as it provided examples of successful, ambitious men, it was clearly not aimed at learning for learning's sake. Although no student who had an "ardent Desire" to learn Latin or Greek would be refused, the study of the classics would not be compulsory.[7] Writing, rhetoric, arithmetic, and accounting were to be taught, with "Regard being had to the several Professions for which they are intended." The history of commerce, particularly of the inventions that served commerce (and the military), would "be useful to all." The physical side of the boys' lives would not be left out: "That to keep them in Health, and to strengthen and render active their Bodies, they be frequently exercis'd in Running, Leaping, Wrestling, and Swimming." The goal of all true learning, Franklin concluded, would be to increase "Inclination join'd with an Ability to serve Mankind, one's Country, Friends and Family." The Academy and Charitable School opened its doors to students in 1751 and became the University of the State of Pennsylvania in 1779. For the last 150 years, Franklin's school has flown under the banner of the University of Pennsylvania.

Although Franklin was a critic of the formalized education of his day, he remained a passionate advocate of lifelong learning. His suspicions about the tendency for institutions of higher education to lose connection to the "real world," the world of commerce and innovation, were joined with his fear that entrenched elites would do their best to stall progress. In Franklin we see two ingredients in the critique of liberal education that have remained potent until our own time: that academics are out of touch and that they tend to serve elites.

The failure of professors to teach their students how to navigate in the real world has been a staple of criticism of colleges in America since the founding of Harvard in 1636. Colleges were accused of insulating students from the kind of learning that experience out in the world would provide, while also giving them an extended period of immaturity in which irresponsibility, incivility, and outright drunkenness prevailed. The usefulness of an education grounded in the classics or in the finer points of theological disputation was not at all evident, and a college degree was often mocked as a luxury that rich families gifted to their sons as a sign of their breeding—not of their capacity to get things done. Nevertheless, by the first half of the nineteenth century the number of colleges had grown significantly, with most of the newer ones founded by disgruntled alumni or teachers from the older institutions. Almost all had some religious affiliation, and they took moral instruction, the development of character, as their most important mission. Whether forward looking or harkening back to some sacred tradition, colleges emphasized pedagogy and morality.[8]

Colleges, whatever their religious affiliation, presented a curriculum that depended on the idea of the seamless integration of knowledge. Morality and science, history and religion, the classics and mathematics all peacefully coexisted as elements in the formation of a cultivated young man. Writing as an advocate for a new Catholic university in Ireland, John Henry Newman stressed that "all branches of knowledge are connected together, because the subject-matter of knowledge is intimately united in itself, as being the acts and the work of the Creator."[9] In the most traditional schools, all students followed the same curriculum, and they enrolled with the same small group of professors. As the number of subjects taught in colleges and universities grew, though, it became clear that not everyone would be able to have the same set of classes. No matter, Newman said in his powerfully influential text; "though they cannot pursue every subject which is open to them, they will be the gainers by living among those and under those who represent the whole circle."[10] As long as the universe of knowledge was a stable circle, colleges and universities would be able to offer access to the Whole.

Throughout the nineteenth century, America was becoming "a nation of colleges." The historian of education David Potts reports that there were ten colleges founded each decade from 1800 to 1830, and sixty came into existence in the 1850s alone![11] New institutions introduced some variations, and this put the traditional model of liberal arts education based in a study of the classics under enormous pressure. Newman's "circle of knowledge" was looking less and less unified. Families of means or of aspiration often wanted their sons to be launched into society by the college they attended, but there were doubts as to whether the content of the education really prepared them for a world of great technological and economic change. Sound familiar? The nation was expanding, and shipping, railroads, communications, and manufacturing were changing rapidly. Could higher education keep up?

In the 1820s there were reforms afoot at several American colleges, all of which aimed to add more modern areas of inquiry and reduce the time spent on rote memorization and on the study of Greek and Latin. Amherst College, just recently founded by a group from Williams College in western Massachusetts, dared to offer a track toward the bachelor's degree that did not depend on the classics at all. Amherst's experiment drew much attention, and enrollment at the college quickly grew. Even at tradition-bound Harvard, the winds of reform were beginning to blow. George Ticknor, who would become Harvard College's first professor of humane letters, returned from a sojourn in Europe determined to modernize what he saw as America's moribund educational structures. "A great and thorough change must take place in its discipline and instruction," he wrote with a real edge, even to "fulfill the purposes of a respectable high school."[12]

Ticknor made a series of recommendations to modernize the old college in Cambridge. He wanted to make the school more accessible to people not pursuing a traditional degree, to reduce the "authorized idleness" of too many weeks of vacation, and he proposed significant changes to the governance and financial sectors of the institution. For our purposes, it is important to note that Ticknor wanted departments, not the university administration, to oversee instruction in their disciplines. Most important, he wanted professors really to teach, not just to determine if their charges had done their studying (which often meant memorizing). "After all," Ticknor wrote, "not one of our colleges is a place for thorough *teaching*; and not one of the better class of them does half of what it might do, by bringing the minds of its instructors to act directly and vigorously on the minds of its pupils."[13] Ticknor wanted students to be able to choose, at least to a certain extent, a course of study, which "would increase the interest of the students in their occupations, and tend to make the knowledge they acquire more valuable for their future purposes in life."[14] He ended his analysis in language that recalls some of today's iconoclastic critics of higher education who call for "disruptive innovation." If elite institutions in higher education don't critically examine their own traditions, "instead of being able to place themselves at the head of the coming changes and directing their course, they will only be the first victims of the spirit of improvement."[15]

There were two crucial responses to the call for curricular modernization in nineteenth-century America. The first was a defense of moderate change through an evolutionary approach to liberal education, and the second, which really took off after the Civil War, was the development of the specialized research university. In the *Yale Report* of 1828 faculty defiantly reject the accusation that the stuffy old American colleges are just teaching in the same mode as their medieval forerunners.[16] Colleges change almost annually, they insist, and alumni just a few years out typically marvel at how different the curriculum looks when they return to campus. Professors are not set in their ways; they continue to refine their teaching practices and the content of the curriculum as part of their own professional work.

The authors of the reports register the criticism that colleges "are not adapted to the spirit and wants of the age; that they will soon be deserted, unless they are better accommodated to the business character of the nation" (6). Today's business-oriented critics of higher education often talk about online learning and e-commerce; the critics in the early nineteenth century were concerned that colleges weren't facilitating industrialization. The Yale authors' rebuttal is that colleges must lay down a foundation on which professional education can be constructed. Without such a foundation, mere professional tools will be less effective and, more important, the lives of professionals will be horribly unbalanced. "Our object is not to teach that which is peculiar to any one of the professions; but to lay the foundation which is common to them all" (14). This foundation is not made up of pillars of facts; it is not made up of memorized texts. The liberal college education provides the *discipline and furniture of the mind*. And it is intellectual discipline that is the more important. Liberal education provides the habits of thinking on which a lifetime of learning will be erected. "The scholar," the report emphasizes, "must form himself by his own exertions" (8). As we would say today, the student must learn how to learn.

The Yale faculty members, however, go on to stress that the study of Greek and Latin is absolutely essential for providing this mental discipline. They repeatedly insist that the institution is open to change, and that it has changed over the years. But they also reject changes that would disrupt the core legacy of the ancient world as the key to the development of intellectual discipline. Their notion of liberal learning is moving toward what will later be called "critical thinking"—habits of mind that are relevant to any inquiry, any professional practice.[17] But liberal learning in the minds of these Yale professors must be based on Greek and Latin. Some "furniture of the mind" was necessary for any civilized home. Without the foundations set by the lessons of the ancients, they insist, disciplined habits of thinking could never be built.

Following the *Yale Reports* and in the years leading up to the Civil War, debates about liberal education focus more on process than on content, though the effort to defend the classics remains a strong undercurrent. Most significant, liberal learning is recast from being an end in itself to being the foundation or preparation for further professional study. Whether one was to pursue engineering or medicine, law or commerce, students were imagined to continue their specialized training on the base of the broad liberal learning they experienced as undergraduates. Colleges were seen as components of universities in which students would receive the benefits of professionalization through more advanced study, and universities were organized not primarily to disseminate knowledge to students but to produce knowledge through research.

Faculty and students working together in research to create knowledge—this was the vision of the university that Americans imported from Germany. German intellectuals themselves held dear an early statement on the essential purpose and organization of universities by the Prussian philologist and ambassador Wilhelm von Humboldt. Although not widely available in print until the late nineteenth century, "On the Inner and Outer Organization of Berlin's Institutions of Higher Knowledge" took on almost mythic status for those reimagining the modern university. Von Humboldt wrote that "institutions of higher knowledge can fully realize their purpose . . . only when they operate according to the pure idea of science." The pursuit of scientific knowledge, in religion, biology, or history, meant endless systematic inquiry and open publication and discussion. This pursuit was what differentiated universities from secondary schools. "Higher institutions are always in the process of research. Thus the relationship between the teacher and the pupil is something utterly unique in the higher institutions. Here the teacher isn't present for the sake of the student alone. Rather, students and teacher come together for the sake of knowledge."[18] The pursuit of knowledge demands freedom—not just freedom from censorship, but also the freedom to organize research in ways that seem to the scholars most appropriate to their object of study. According to this idea of the university, the desire to make practical use of the fruits of research must always take a back seat to protecting the ongoing pursuit of knowledge for its own sake. Otherwise, those looking for the practical fruits will kill the very tree that produces those fruits in the first place. The tree of knowledge—science itself—must be allowed to grow in its own way. "The crucial challenge is," von Humboldt wrote, "upholding the principle whereby science is seen as something that must be pursued endlessly" (34).

The American research university was built on this idea of endless inquiry in a context of freedom and collaboration. But much had to be cleared away so that the construction could begin. Key to this effort was Charles Eliot, who served as president of Harvard for forty years. In some ways he was an unlikely choice to lead our oldest college. Although he had a Harvard degree, his appointment as an instructor in the sciences wasn't renewed. After traveling in Europe and visiting its universities, he returned to a professorship at the young Massachusetts Institute of Technology. In an 1869 *Atlantic Monthly* article entitled "The New Education," Eliot posed a provocative parental question to which Harvard and almost every American college would have to respond: "What can I do with my boy? I can afford, and am glad, to give him the best training to be had. I should be proud to have him turn out a preacher or a learned man; but I don't think he has the making of that in him. I want to give him a practical education; one that will prepare him, better than I was prepared, to follow my business or any other active calling."[19] Eliot imagines a father trying to find an education that will prepare his son for the future in a rapidly changing new world. "He will not believe that the same methods which trained some boys well for the life of fifty or one hundred years ago are applicable to his son; for the reason, that the kind of man which he wants his son to make did not exist in all the world fifty years ago."

Universities must change because they must be the best expression of a changing society. Don't expect professors to change them, though, Eliot warns. Spending your life as a

teacher makes one an "unsafe witness in matters of education." Changes come from the fields in which knowledge
is being made, the sciences, and they should help initiate
changes across universities too beholden to a classical
model. Eliot means to shake up the model by bringing
more and more subjects into the curriculum. "It cannot be
said too loudly or too often, that no subject of human inquiry can be out of place in the programme of a real university," he wrote. "It is only necessary that every subject
should be taught at the university on a higher plane than
elsewhere." Some scholars will think that somebody else's
field isn't worth teaching, but for Eliot, "it is impossible to
be too catholic in this matter." By being more catholic, by
teaching more subjects, the good would drive out the bad.

Eliot became president of Harvard less than a year after
his essay appeared in the *Atlantic Monthly*. Within his first
decade in office, there was a significant increase in the mo-
mentum of reform in American higher education. The
German model of the research university was steadily gain-
ing more adherents who attempted to graft that model onto
the American collegiate experience. Even the first president of the research-oriented Johns Hopkins University,
Daniel Gilman, made sure to say that the freedom of inquiry in advanced work was only possible after students had
had a collegiate experience, which "gives a liberal and substantial foundation on which the university instruction
may be wisely built."[20] In his inaugural speech Gilman
built on the themes that von Humboldt had laid down decades before in Berlin. The modern university must be

unfettered by dogma and tradition. "If we would maintain a university, great freedom must be allowed both to teachers and scholars," intoned Gilman. "This involves freedom of methods to be employed by the instructors on the one hand, and on the other, freedom of courses to be selected by the students."

In an American context, and perhaps with a nod to the *Yale Reports*, Gilman recognizes that this freedom is only possible because of the "collegiate discipline" that students and teachers had already internalized before beginning advanced university work. Colleges were appropriate for the Republic in its infancy, but the modernizing nation needed universities that produced research—much as American industry was producing products for an expanding market. The American university would emphasize what has come to be called the scholar-teacher model, one in which researchers are said to be more effective because they are instructors, and instructors are said to be more compelling because they are actively creating knowledge as researchers. Advanced university work would be specialized, to be sure, but "the best scholars will almost invariably be those who make special attainments on the foundation of a broad and liberal culture."

Gilman, like Eliot at Harvard, was well aware that critics would say that American institutions would lose touch with the moral basis of education if they emulated the German university. Specialized knowledge was all well and good, but the pursuit of narrow technical expertise could produce a breed of narrow technical men who did not know how to deal with the world beyond their particular specialty. Even in launching Johns Hopkins, Gilman reminded his audience of the roots of the American university in liberal learning: "The object of the university is to develop character — to make men. It misses its aim if it produces learned pedants, or simple artisans, or cunning sophists, or pretentious practitioners. Its purport is not so much to impart knowledge to the pupils, as whet the appetite, exhibit methods, develop powers, strengthen judgment, and invigorate the intellectual and moral forces. It should prepare for the service of society a class of students who will be wise, thoughtful, progressive guides in whatever department of work or thought they may be engaged." Gilman insisted on the continuity of the university with the college, and the link between them was liberal education. For him this meant increasing the capacity of the students and faculty to learn through research. Von Humboldt had emphasized that inquiry never ended, and the American university aimed to create a culture in which faculty and students alike would develop the habits of mind that would pursue knowledge "in whatever department of work or thought they may be engaged." The point was not technical — learning how to perform a particular experimental or scholarly technique. The point was liberal, by which he meant preparing "wise, thoughtful, progressive guides" who would contribute to society and not just to their own disciplines through their ongoing search for knowledge.

The American research university that developed after the Civil War did not attempt to replace colleges but to add an additional level of education to what had been available to undergraduates. At Harvard Eliot was very explicit about this, since in addition to establishing graduate and professional programs of advanced research he made the undergraduate degree a prerequisite for them. This would eventually become the norm across the land. And through the end of the nineteenth century, sometimes echoing Cardinal Newman, university leaders often appealed to the unity of knowledge that was the hallmark of the collegiate experience. In the colleges, ethics, aesthetics, and knowledge were integrated with one another, and modern universities "sought to preserve one of the key values of the classical college: the unity of moral and intellectual purpose."[21]

But what would provide the unifying force that would bring together moral and intellectual purpose? In order to promote freedom of inquiry, universities had to be free of interference from the state and from religion, two institutional forces that had traditionally imposed unity on what was taught. Insofar as the schools were set up with private endowments, they had some real protection against government interference. In any case, government officials after the Civil War saw an investment in scientific research as a national imperative, and they didn't attempt to control the inquiry of scientists in the same ways that they strove to frame the work of the other disciplines. As scientific work became increasingly specialized in universities, researchers tended to avoid broad debates about the meaning of education and the formation of character. This was in sharp contrast to religious institutions. Many of the colleges and universities of the land had some religious affiliation, and many argued it was this connection to religion that provided a foundation for the educational missions of the schools. But in the last decades of the nineteenth century there was a drumbeat for disaffiliation of universities from any particular branch of Protestantism. James McCosh, president of Princeton, swam against the tide in arguing that religion was too important to be left as one elective among many. McCosh thought that institutions should make a strong commitment to a creed that produced a framework for learning. But Harvard's Eliot made what turned out to be the compelling argument that an a priori commitment to a denomination's principles was an obvious impediment to free inquiry. A man of science "pursues truth eagerly . . . without due regard to its possible effects on venerable associations, precious feelings, or traditional sanctities."[22] Religion could be studied like any other subject area; it would no longer be immune to inquiry. When studied like any other subject, however, religion no longer provided the force to hold together the community of inquiring minds.

When Ezra Cornell declaimed at the end of the 1860s that he would create a school "where any person can find instruction in any study," he charted a path in sync with the increase in population and the expansion of fields of knowledge. The expansion and diffusion of knowledge took precedence over any effort to discover its unifying principles. The men who built research universities in the last decades of the nineteenth century were convinced that a commitment to inquiry itself would provide all the commonality necessary to hold a community of scholars together. There need not be an overarching shared moral framework, and no one discipline need guide the others so long as all scholars recognized they shared a commitment to the pursuit of truth. At least that was the hope. In fact, faculty members and students found it increasingly difficult to have any spirit of joint endeavor as institutions grew in size and scope—and this was true even in the institutes or separate schools under a university's umbrella. At Harvard, Eliot continued to profess that through liberal learning, "it is possible for the young to get actual experience of all the principal methods of thought."[23] The challenge—one of scale, method, and content—was to reconcile this broad mandate with the reality of increasingly crowded and increasingly specialized research-oriented universities. The scale of universities was changing precipitously. As the number of students and professors grew, it became increasingly unlikely that someone studying poetry would have the chance to benefit from interaction with someone studying chemistry. The scale of specific schools or departments within a university was large enough to provide the basis for specialized communities. As one moved into the early twentieth century, research methods across the disciplines no longer seemed to share salient features. The situation became even more problematic as particular methodologies in the sciences claimed to set the standard for rational, objective study—a standard that many fields didn't recognize as their own.

Finally, as graduate students searched for original research topics in increasingly specialized subdisciplines, it seemed only other academic professionals in the same subdiscipline could see the worth of the work being undertaken. What did broad, liberal education mean if even members of university communities couldn't figure out what was happening on the other side of their own campuses?

William James, hired by the great university reformer Eliot, points to the dangers of overspecialization just as the research university began to hit its stride. He pokes fun at the German model, which aims only "to turn the student into an instrument for advancing scientific discovery." James asks us to consider whether we really want to emulate a system in which students can go off on their own and find "some little pepper-corn of new truth worthy of being added to the store of extant human information on that subject."[24] Were those ambitious goals to grasp the unity of Truth and prepare well-rounded citizens giving way now to the production of miniscule research nuggets? American institutions of higher education were modernizing, but why would one call this progress? Would the pursuit of specialization drive liberal learning from the most "advanced" universities?

The model of the specialized university in which advanced research and professional work was grafted onto a broad undergraduate course of study dominated by electives would eventually become the standard for much of American higher education. But in the second half of the nineteenth century there were other institutional experiments that would have important reverberations throughout the twentieth century and beyond. Although religion receded in importance in most elite schools in the Northeast, dozens of denominational colleges did spring up in other parts of the country. Religiously oriented institutions developed their own versions of what should count as liberal learning. In addition, the Morrill Act, signed into law in 1862 and augmented in 1890, facilitated the creation of well-funded universities in various parts of the country in order "to teach such branches of learning as are related to agriculture and the mechanic arts." These state-run land-grant colleges and universities were to provide a utilitarian education, though "without excluding other scientific and classical studies." Thus, American universities, unlike their European counterparts, attempted to place vocational learners side by side with those studying traditional academic subjects. But even those supporting utilitarian studies within universities added that they aimed "to promote the liberal and practical education of the industrial classes in the several pursuits and professions in life."[25] In America, liberal education was not completely segregated from agriculture and the mechanical arts because of the insistence that liberal learning benefited the individual and society regardless of one's occupation. At least that has been the case until recently.

The second half of the nineteenth century was also a time when higher education for women grew enormously. Throughout the first decades of the century, the relatively few women who had access to education were taught at academies, seminaries, and a few colleges. Their teachers often went along with the Enlightenment notion that education led to autonomy, but given that the social goal for most of these girls was marriage, the notion of autonomy was attenuated by the demand that they obey their husbands. Perhaps that's why many young women educated in academies developed different marriage patterns than those who did not attend school. Graduates of the academies tended to marry later, and there was a larger percentage than in the general population that didn't marry at all.[26] In the decades before the Civil War many used their education to become teachers themselves. In the aftermath of the great conflict, women's colleges were founded that would have a notable impact on the conception of educational opportunity throughout the country: Vassar (1865), Wellesley (1875), Smith (1875), and Bryn Mawr (1884). All these schools aspired to offer women a liberal education at least the equal of the institutions available to men. As Smith's president put it, evoking the tradition of liberal learning with which we are now familiar: "The college is not intended to fit woman for any particular sphere or profession but to develop by the most carefully devised means all her intellectual capacities, so that she may be a more perfect woman in any position."[27] By insisting that women need not be restricted to "any particular sphere" decades before they even had the right to vote, women's colleges devoted to liberal education were a dynamic, progressive force in this country.

The percentage of women in the total population of college students rose from 21 percent in 1870 to over 47 percent in 1920. It has continued to rise ever since. This was also the period in which liberal education was being redefined in relation to the emerging research university, and women's colleges played a role in that redefinition. The early women's colleges were likely to retain the more classically oriented curriculum—having only recently been able to offer this education, perhaps they were more reluctant to change it. Traditional subjects seemed more likely to attract women students, and by the first decade of the twentieth century, classics professors already had begun complaining about the feminization of their field. The male students were choosing other electives, and professors of Greek (who were likely to have been taught that women couldn't learn the language) stood in front of classrooms filled with young women. Both genders, though, were enrolling in the increasingly popular social sciences. But there was a difference in what liberal education meant for young men and women: for men, liberal education was the first step toward professionalization. For women, it was learning for its own sake, since most professions were still closed to them. Still, professors usually spoke about the curriculum as if it were solely for men. In the world of higher education women were still an anomaly.[28]

The pious rhetoric around liberal education always emphasized that it was learning for its own sake. If that were true, then the curriculum for men and women could be pretty much the same. But if men were really being educated so as to pursue professional expertise and women were learning to assume their place in the home, then they would need different educational itineraries. But could these both be called liberal?

M. Carey Thomas was a major intellectual and administrative force in favor of women's liberal and professional education at the turn of the century. The second president of Bryn Mawr College, she was a staunch advocate of a college curriculum steeped in the classics, but she also led the first women's college that had graduate departments. She had attended Cornell University as an undergraduate before doing graduate work at Johns Hopkins, the University of Leipzig, and the University of Zurich, where she was awarded a Ph.D. in linguistics. Thomas wanted women's education to uphold the highest traditional standards—which men were already changing. Although plenty of other schools were integrating home economics into women's undergraduate studies, Thomas made a powerful argument on behalf of a more traditional curriculum that would prepare women (as well as men) for advanced professional work. She recognized that most women after college would have different destinies than most men, but for that very reason she thought it important that they have a common educational background: "[Women's] college education should be the same as men's, not only because there is, I believe, but one best education, but because men and women are to live and work together as comrades and dear friends and married friends and lovers, and because their effectiveness and happiness and the welfare of the generation to come after them will be vastly increased if their college education has given them the same intellectual training and the same scholarly and moral ideals."[29] This notion of liberal education as a common culture would resonate deeply throughout the twentieth century, even as pressures on what counted as "common" grew more intense with the recognition of the country's broad diversity.

In the first decades of the twentieth century, American higher education would grow in size and scope. As a larger percentage of the population was finishing high school, an increasing number of young men and women began to think of a college or university education as a pathway to adulthood and the working world. This did not mean that significantly greater numbers of Americans dreamed of pursuing advanced research or of becoming professors. But more and more were buying into the notion that some college "experience" would be a preparation for the kind of knowledge they would need to be successful in the new economy and to participate more fully in modern society. These changes in the culture and demographics of American education led to two very different responses. On the one hand, major cities developed universities or colleges to teach the new population, often immigrants or their children, who wanted to continue their education beyond secondary school. The College of the City of New York, to take the most impressive example, enrolled more than twenty-four thousand students in the 1920s. On the other hand, well-established schools felt threatened by the tide of newcomers eager to learn. Junior colleges and municipal institutions might be just fine for the masses, but the more established institutions would start to define themselves by their selectivity. Prestige came through the numbers of students to whom one refused admission. Selectivity often meant that schools would create particular filters to ensure that the "social homogeneity" or "appropriate learning environment" would be maintained. This was often a code for ensuring that the college experience would not be polluted by Jews or other minority groups.

Meanwhile, the professoriate was growing, too, as were the professional societies that conferred distinction on scholars in any number of fields. The Modern Language Association, the American Historical Association, and the disciplinary societies in the sciences all came of age as the nineteenth century came to an end. Professors at elite universities were developing the standards according to which work in their respective fields would be judged across the country. Published expertise in a specialty allowed one to be evaluated not just by local colleagues but by "the field" at large. The American Association of University Professors was established in 1915 to defend "academic freedom," the freedom to pursue research without interference from nonscholars. The professor as creator of new knowledge was becoming firmly entrenched as a core idea in American colleges and universities. New knowledge, however, did not necessarily connote liberal learning. Indeed, given the intensification of specialization, what was esteemed as an intellectual advancement in one field was likely to seem irrelevant or opaque to other fields. Expertise, not breadth of learning, was the ticket to professional advancement for professors. Universities competed for faculty of note, and so, as historian of education Robert Geiger has remarked, one was more likely to find a Jewish physicist at Princeton than a Jewish student.

By the 1920s, as a reaction to the intensification of specialization, on the one hand, and the decline of religious culture in universities, on the other, colleges were increasingly emphasizing the importance of what was learned outside the classroom. The college "experience" was not just a sum of the lectures heard, seminars attended, or research conducted; "student life" was said to be a vital component of what was learned in the undergraduate years. The model for this was the residential college, promoting the four years of work toward a bachelor's degree as a way of life that encouraged habits of learning. Whether dormitories were built or not (and many were, sometimes with government support), the "collegiate way" became core to postsecondary education after World War I. Rather than emphasizing the autonomy or self-reliance of undergraduates, higher education assumed an increasingly paternalist function. The residential collegiate way allowed for a transition to adult participation in mainstream middle-class culture.[30]

The residential collegiate experience has attracted enormous devotion from students and alumni whose great affection for their undergraduate years was not in any way compromised by their lack of passion for the intricacies of advanced research work pursued by the new brand of expert professors. This devotion would become increasingly important to colleges and universities whose growth would depend on donations from alumni. Fraternities, sports teams, eating clubs . . . all these trappings of contemporary university life developed in the 1920s alongside the heightened intellectual investment in specialized research. But for most undergraduates, it was not the heightened intellectual investment that came to define their college experience.

Specialized research, however, would increasingly dominate graduate education in the twentieth century, and it was in graduate school that professors received their training. Thus their ability (and often their desire) to participate in the "collegiate ideal" diminished as their professional aspirations rose. In response, university administrators developed advising programs to assign professors some formal role in guiding students through their first years of study (although many schools asked for faculty volunteers). But the professor who emerged from years of specialized graduate study might not have much interest in or aptitude for advising college students. The professional pedantry linked to poor teaching was also linked to poor advising.[31] This was already being widely discussed in the 1920s! That's when schools began to hire professional student affairs staff to run freshman orientation programs and other initiatives that would help burnish the allure of the collegiate ideal.

Throughout the twentieth century, undergraduate education at universities and colleges has come to be thought of more as a way of life that develops general habits than as a set of courses that develops particular skills. In this way, the cocurricular and extracurricular dimensions of campus life have become part of what counts as liberal education. Universities have struggled to control what goes on outside of the classroom for centuries, and students have fought back against control with all the tools and energies of youth. Remember Jefferson's worries about student drinking! For generations, students have demanded liberties on campus impervious to any interventions by the faculty. To bolster the claims for the importance of student culture, their activities were recoded as being part of the world of learning—not just the world of leisure. Attributing additional importance to activities outside the classroom had benefits for students, alumni, and administrators, providing some counterweight to the growth of specialized research. Intercollegiate sports became an important vehicle for building school spirit (and increasing alumni donations), and soon administrators were describing them as educative activities that build character— discipline, teamwork, leadership. Residential arrangements on campus became a focus for undergraduates and their families, and they were said to facilitate peer-to-peer learning, modeling free discussion and debate. Student newspapers, glee clubs, literary societies . . . all would be brought under the increasingly important administrative function of "student life." And for many members of the "campus community," this is where liberal education migrated: away from the specialized research interests of ambitious faculty and toward the community-building enterprises of an increasingly energized (but also regulated) student culture.

Liberal education remained a core American value in the first half of the twentieth century, but a value under enormous pressure from demographic expansion and the development of more consistent public schooling. The increase in the population considering postsecondary education was dramatic. In 1910 only 9 percent of students received a high school diploma; by 1940 it was 50 percent.[32] For the great majority of those who went on to college, that education would be primarily vocational, whether in agriculture, business, or the mechanical arts. But as we have seen, even in vocationally oriented programs there was a desire to develop a liberal curriculum — a curriculum that would provide an educational base on which one could continue to learn — rather than just skills for the next job. In addition to these social changes, within the academy itself the field of play had changed with the clear ascendancy of the sciences. Discoveries in physics, chemistry, and biology did not seem to depend on the moral, political, or cultural views of the researchers, and these discoveries had a powerful impact on industry, the military, and health care. Specialized scientific research at universities produced tangible results, so why not get nonacademic groups to adopt their methodologies so as to transform private industry and the public sphere? Given the progress in scientific fields, more people were asking whether the traditional ideas of liberal education provided a foundation for this work, or whether they were merely archaic vestiges of a mode of education that should be left behind.

In reaction to this ascendancy of the sciences, many literature departments reimagined themselves as realms of value and heightened subjectivity, as opposed to so-called value-free, objective work. These "new humanists" of the 1920s saw the study of literature as an antidote to the spiritual vacuum left by hyperspecialization. Rather than pursuing the possibilities of rigorous philological or linguistic work, they emphasized that spiritual growth and self-understanding were the core of humanistic study. The notion that the study of literature led to a greater appreciation of cultural significance and a personal search for meaning spilled over into other areas of the curriculum. Historians and philosophers emphasized the synthetic dimensions of their endeavors, pointing out how they were able to bring ideas and facts together to help students create meaning. Creating meaning was tied to a moral education—not just a scientific one. In addition, arts instruction at this time was reimagined as part of the development of a student's ability to explore great works that expressed the highest values of a civilization. Artists were brought to campuses to inspire students rather than to teach them the nuances of their craft. During this interwar period a liberal education surely included the sciences, but many educators insisted that it not be reduced to them.[33]

Thus, despite the pressures of social change and of the compelling results of specialized research, there remained strong support for the notion that liberal education and learning for its own sake were essential for an educated citizenry. And rather than restrict a nonvocational education

to established elites, some saw this broad teaching as a vehicle for ensuring commonality in a country of immigrants.
The somewhat paradoxical notion was that inquiry without
prejudice would give rise to basic democratic values
(because these "values" were not mere prejudices). Young
people would be socialized to a specifically American way
of life by learning to think for themselves. By the 1930s, an
era when ideological indoctrination and fanaticism were
thought to be the opposite of this way of life, a liberal education was acclaimed as key to the protection of free citizens. Here is the president of Harvard, James Bryant
Conant, speaking to undergraduates just two years after
Hitler had come to power in Germany:

> To my mind, one of the most important aspects of a
> college education is that it provides a vigorous stimu-
> lus to independent thinking. . . . The desire to know
> more about the different sides of a question, a craving
> to understand something of the opinions of other
> peoples and other times mark the educated man.
> Education should not put the mind in a strait-jacket
> of conventional formulas but should provide it with
> the nourishment on which it may unceasingly ex-
> pand and grow. Think for yourselves! Absorb knowl-
> edge wherever possible and listen to the opinions of
> those more experienced than yourself, but don't let
> any one do your thinking for you.[34]

This was the 1930s version of liberal learning, and it evoked
Jefferson's autonomy and Emerson's self-reliance. Our

independence, our freedom, depended on not letting anyone else do our thinking for us. And that demanded learning for its own sake; it demanded a liberal education.

As World War II ended, a committee of Harvard professors organized by Conant released a far-reaching declaration of ambition for American education. *General Education in a Free Society* presented both a philosophy of education and a series of recommendations for how American citizens might be prepared to think for themselves in the postwar era. The committee members used the term "general education," it seems, because they felt that "liberal education" applied too narrowly to just college instruction. General education was a term that colleges had used, too, often to mark that "education should get at something bigger than any single discipline."[35] Columbia had started its general education classes in the wake of World War I in an attempt to link the study of historically significant works with problems in the contemporary world, and several schools instituted similar classes to make the college curriculum more immediately relevant.[36] These would be "great books" classes that studied texts not owned by any one discipline—but texts that retained a powerful relevance to life beyond the campus.

The combination of time-tested greatness and contemporary relevance was key for Conant's very distinguished committee. Its members were interested in providing a national framework for thinking about education in the wake of fascism's defeat and new threats from communism. In their vision of a modern, free society, education should provide individual opportunity, and it should provide the grounds for social cohesion: "Taken as a whole, education seeks to do two things: help young persons fulfill the unique, particular functions in life which it is in them to fulfill, and fit them so far as it can for those common spheres which, as citizens and heirs of a joint culture, they will share with others."[37] Conant was concerned that the "particular functions" that might be assigned to young people would be dictated by the economic conditions of their families, and that over the generations this would result in ever-greater economic inequality. Such inequality would make it increasingly difficult for citizens to believe they had a "joint culture," and it would make the country more vulnerable to social unrest based on class division. In a pair of articles written for the *Atlantic Monthly*, Conant laid out his twofold Jeffersonian approach to defeating entrenched inequality.[38] His first idea was straightforward but still radical for a university president: the regular redistribution of wealth so that one generation could not pass on its privileges to another. Conant thought that the American educated elite would be public spirited enough to accept an estate tax that would allow government to prevent economic winners from passing on their advantages to the next generation. The second idea was a robust public school system that would enable children from any background to find their way to a ladder of opportunity. He advocated the development of sophisticated testing so as to discover capacities that might not be visible to current elites. Colleges and universities should admit those with the highest aptitude rather than the best connections, and he argued that we needed good testing and substantial financial aid to make this possible. Recall that Jefferson had called this "raking the rubbish" in hopes of finding those with talent. Conant's rake would eventually be called the SAT.[39]

Education would make students into citizens, Conant emphasized, "but, more important still, they must be equipped to step on to the first rung of whatever ladder of opportunity seemed most appropriate. And an appropriate ladder must be found for each one of a diverse group of students." General education for Conant, like liberal education for Jefferson, was meant to counterbalance the negative by-products of the inequality that would necessarily develop in a society that prized opportunity.[40] Jefferson feared an "unnatural aristocracy" based on lucky imbeciles who happened to inherit family wealth. Conant feared communist activists who would exploit class divisions to incite a revolution that would end in a totalitarian state of bureaucratic equality. "The root idea of general education," Conant's committee wrote, "is as a balance and counterpoise to the forces which divide group from group" (14). A curriculum for a free society would aim to enable the talented to thrive while also expanding the horizons of "the ordinary boys." "It could pursue the two goals simultaneously: give scope to ability and raise the average. Nor are these two goals so far apart, if human beings are capable of common sympathies" (35). Forming common sympathy out of diversity—that very American challenge was the challenge of general education.

The Harvard committee's report, dubbed the *Red Book*, discusses the major obstacles to the development of general education, mainly the diversity of the students and of the material to be taught. People in modern America lived in such different circumstances and hailed from such different backgrounds. Furthermore, not only were science and technology advancing at a breathtaking pace but such distinct methods were used in these newly emerging fields. For the people and for the subjects, what would be the unifying factors, and who would decide what most people should know? The professorial committee examined some of the traditional vehicles for answering these questions, but in the end it focused on the importance of heritage and experimentation. The first would provide the key ingredients for social cohesion, while the second would allow for incremental progress. Experimental initiatives that proved successful would themselves become part of our heritage. The committee did not try to argue that some works are obviously superior to others, only that Western society had recognized particular works as part of its tradition for a long time. Appealing to the reverential dimension of the rhetorical framework for education, it argued that the books traditionally read by the educated elite should be the books we learn to read together. "The task of modern democracy is to preserve the ancient ideal of liberal education and to extend it as far as possible to all the members of the community" (53). In a nod to contemporary scientific studies and the philosophical framework for education, the committee affirmed that general education in a modern democracy would be complemented by specific studies that have immediate utility, or at least that generate potentially productive experiments. Reverence for great works should complement powerful inquiry that generates new knowledge.

The synthesis recommended in the *Red Book* was meant to address the needs for acculturation and skill building in high schools as well as the requirements for advanced work in colleges and universities. The professors recognized the difficulties of finding a common heritage in the changing populations of high schools in different parts of the country. After all, some were isolated rural schools with small numbers of students expected to work on farms, while others were large urban schools whose students were being swept up in the newest dimensions of the economy. The *Red Book* authors also recognized the challenges of finding professors to teach courses of general value in a university system that aimed to produce specialized experts. "The undergraduate in a college receives his teaching from professors who, in their turn, have been trained in graduate schools. And the latter are dominated by the ideal of specialization. Learning now is diversified and parceled into a myriad of specialties" (56). The triumph of "specialism" is not confined to universities, however. Our entire society, the committee noted, now depends on technical expertise, and in this context liberal learning is more important than ever. "I am in peculiar need of a kind of Sagacity," notes the *Red Book*, "by which to distinguish the expert from the quack . . . the aim of general education may be defined as that of providing the broad critical sense by which to recognize competence in any field" (54). A "broad critical sense" is the Harvard team's version of the "disciplined thinking" in the *Yale Report* of 1828. For both, liberal education is a vehicle for counteracting the centripetal forces of modernization. Specialization is the modern form of fragmentation, and fragmentation will result in inequality that eventually breeds social unrest and worse. Liberal education (and its public face, general education) was an attempt to offer a "counterpoise" to this modern tendency, a resource of commonality for citizens and scholars alike. The *Red Book* went on to specify the "traits of mind" that would be enhanced by this commonality: effective thinking, communication, the making of relevant judgments, and the discrimination of values (73). All citizens needed these traits of mind, and by teaching a range of subjects based in traditional culture or contemporary experimentation, one would be able to develop the self-awareness that went along with these traits. At least that was the hope: "To the extent that a student becomes aware of the methods he is using, and critically conscious of his presuppositions, he learns to transcend his specialty and generates a liberal outlook in himself" (64).

Transcending one's particularity in the public sphere, going beyond one's private or class interests, is a perennial challenge in a republic heavily invested in individual rights and liberties. Key to meeting this challenge is "common sympathy" with one's neighbors or fellow citizens. For a university's faculty, this challenge took the form of transcending one's department, the bureaucratic incarnation of one's specialization. The students, as we noted above, were encouraged to develop common sympathies via athletics and other student activities that aimed to generate school spirit. What would give the professors a sense of belonging to the university as a whole? Despite myriad efforts to define areas of general education, distribution requirements, or essential capabilities in higher education throughout the 1950s and 1960s, the challenge of maintaining common academic goals in the era of specialization proved too daunting for most universities that had come to prize research success in their faculty members. Even when a university required, as the *Red Book* recommended, general courses in the humanities, social sciences, and natural sciences, the tendency of the departments was to generate more and more specialized classes. After all, that's what the faculty were trained to teach.[41]

The two challenges that Harvard's *Red Book* recognized for creating a sense of common purpose through education — the diversity of people and the diversity of knowledge — have shadowed discussions of liberal learning from Jefferson until our own day. The specialized research university, with professional programs grafted onto a collegiate experience, was a response to the challenges, but it also exacerbated them. The professionalization of the faculty was built on the notion that the university should be free to follow the quest for knowledge wherever it might take the researcher. This meant freedom from governmental, religious, or commercial interference in research, but also freedom from the specific intellectual and social requirements of students. It's no accident that when schools begin competing for prestigious faculty, one of the first things they offer is a reduction in the number of students the professor will be asked to teach.

Although the *Red Book* was clearly a response to the important changes that had already taken place in universities in the first half of the twentieth century, the thirty years following World War II "were possibly the most tumultuous in the history of American higher education."[42] The G.I. Bill enabled millions of returning soldiers to enroll in colleges, and the proportion of young people pursuing undergraduate degrees tripled between 1940 and 1970. The expansion affected all sectors. Graduate programs expanded dramatically, as did community colleges. There seemed to be a broad commitment to the general education version of liberal learning, which meant that even vocationally oriented programs often strengthened their offerings in the arts and sciences. Large public institutions became even bigger, while private universities became both more selective in admissions and more devoted than ever to supporting the research of the faculty. The federal government became the major investor in faculty research after the Russian *Sputnik* launch in 1957, and this included support for facilities and for graduate students. Historians have described a "golden age" for education as federal and state support and increasing enrollments came together to pump enormous amounts of energy into the sector.[43]

During this period of expansion there was broad acknowledgment that universities produced knowledge while educating millions in ways that enhanced cultural literacy and preparation for the professions. The faculty's control of the curriculum and of hiring and promoting within its ranks was all but complete. This was what Reisman and Jencks described as the "professionalization of academic life" in their 1968 book *The Academic Revolution*. At those elite universities that set the paradigm for performance, professors controlled research and devoted considerable time and care to monitoring its quality. They often belonged to professional associations and aspired to publish in "refereed" journals—publications that tap into the expertise of certified specialists to determine if work is worthy of publication. But most American colleges and universities have not produced groundbreaking research. Their mission is teaching. Who monitors the quality of teaching? The other revolution that was occurring when Reisman and Jencks published their book was the student revolution. This is not the place to discuss its many causes and effects, but we should note that at many schools the students took control of monitoring the quality of teaching. This sometimes happened in stages, with students disseminating informal rankings of professors as part of the campus culture. As with other cocurricular activities, universities eventually found ways to formalize (and, to some extent, sanitize) these processes. Anonymous student evaluations of classes are now obligatory across the country at most colleges and universities. This was one place where the faculty could be

persuaded to cede power to students. Sure, faculty committees and university officials still make decisions about
whether a professor is a good enough teacher to be hired or
promoted. But the great bulk of the information they use to
determine the quality of teaching is the satisfaction of the
students as expressed on surveys. In his introduction to
the 2002 edition of *The Academic Revolution*, Jencks puts it
this way: "So instead of giving students what grownups
think the students need, most teaching institutions are under considerable pressure to give students what they want."[44]
Since giving the students what they want doesn't have any
impact on the professor's research agenda, at many schools
this practice doesn't seem to have impacted the faculty's
sense of control of what they regard as the academic core of
the institution.

The combination of faculty control of specialized research agendas and student control over the evaluation of
teaching changed the political dynamic on many campuses after the end of the Vietnam War. Former student pro-
testors who became professors often had great sympathy for
the political demands of undergraduates, as long as these
didn't interfere with the guild's control over research. On
most campuses, it seemed that professors and students
could agree that they favored "choice." As *The Study of
Education at Stanford* put it in 1968, "The faculty member should be free to pursue his intellectual interests wherever they may lead him. The student, other things being
equal, should be similarly free."[45] A deep commitment to
general education is impossible in a context in which

faculty and students prize above all their ability to teach and study what they want.[46] This was the latest extension of the "elective" system that Eliot had championed at Harvard at the beginning of the twentieth century. Some schools (Columbia, Chicago, and St. John's, to name a few) maintained a core set of classes that everybody had to take, but these were usually just a handful of courses that were often taught by teachers without regular, full-time faculty appointments. Distribution requirements of the kind that the *Red Book* authors favored—a little science, a little humanities, a little social science—were the gestures schools made to the ideal of the "well-rounded student." This allowed faculty to continue to offer classes that connected to their research, no matter how specific, and it allowed students to choose their favorite topics or the most popular teachers. Liberal learning seemed to be thought of as access to a smorgasbord of specific topics, and one could add to those topics willy-nilly. This last point was important because as the student body grew more diverse, it demanded that the courses offered reflected more than just the Euro-American-dominated curriculum that had ruled in the past (particularly in the humanities and social sciences). Universities should add classes into the curriculum concerning previously marginalized groups (especially when these reflected popular research areas), and students would vote with their feet.

Freedom to teach what you wanted combined with freedom to study what you wanted came to define the academic experience of a great many teachers and students at elite research universities and liberal arts colleges by the 1970s. There were requirements within specializations—biologists had to know certain things, and so did economists and historians—but only "distribution" defined the curriculum as a whole. The guild of tenured professors within a field determined which research was worthy of recognition, and the marketplace of student satisfaction determined which classes and teachers were "outstanding." As for the mission of the university as a whole, one could have only the vaguest of hopes that it would emerge from some invisible hand working through the choices of students and faculty.

It was this context that gave rise to (and was the target of) Alan Bloom's *The Closing of the American Mind* (1987). The book was a provocative (many would say infuriating) critique of how our universities had become a symptom of some of the worst features of democratic (that is, for Bloom, commercial) life, a symptom that exhibited a self-righteous relativism that obscured under the cloak of tolerance its inability to address seriously questions of truth and value. Bloom, who came of age studying with Leo Strauss at the University of Chicago near the end of World War II, railed against the culture of the professors and the students, both of which he thought had lost the ability to exercise their powers of recognition and judgment. Like Strauss, he saw a disabling relativism sapping the intellectual and moral fiber of the West. Real greatness and evil had become invisible in a land where only tolerance seemed to matter. If the only virtue recognized in education is well-roundedness, Bloom thundered, students are never confronted with fundamental tensions or choices in life. When everyone is "entitled to his or her own opinion," there is no truth—and so nobody's opinion really matters. Everyone was happily (or at least self-righteously) locked in silos in the land of academic pluralism. Scientists pursued the immediate objects of their research regardless of its wider implications (which would not be considered subject to scientific analysis). Literary critics no longer found it palatable to defend a canon of great books that students ought to read to orient themselves to the enduring questions of human existence. Even philosophers were more interested in showing their technical expertise in logic and linguistics than they were in illuminating traditional conflicts of private and public justice, social inequality, or natural right. For Bloom, the happy relativism that grew out of America's idiosyncratic combination of historicism and Nietzschean perspectivism left us unable to consider essential questions—the questions that Western culture had pondered in academies, monasteries, colleges, and universities for centuries. "The university's task is thus well defined, if not easy to carry out or even keep in mind," wrote Bloom. "It is, in the first place, always to maintain the permanent questions front and center. This it does primarily by preserving—by keeping alive—the works of those who best addressed these questions."[47] But in the modern research university, there was no longer any consensus that there were "permanent questions," let alone what these might be. Nor was there any consensus among faculty members about which works best addressed issues of permanent import. This was not something one covered anymore during one's professional education in graduate school.

Bloom had a storehouse of axes to grind, but of most interest here is his claim that the notion of "liberal education" became vacuous when it was joined to contemporary relativism. For him, we had simply eased into relativist attitudes through our acceptance of the importance of history and culture. Different historical epochs or cultures, we had come to assume, could only be understood internally, not according to any natural or philosophic standard. In education this historicism led to the assumption that variety, any variety, would produce a general education, because no specific cultural product could be said to be superior to others. Pushpin, as the founder of utilitarianism Jeremy Bentham put it, is as good as music or poetry. This was why the same distribution requirement might be satisfied by a course in Shakespeare or by a course in amateur filmmaking in Brooklyn. Commonsense civility had led us to a place where we were afraid to make any judgments about the merits of the material studied because to do so might offend somebody. "It is not the immorality of relativism that I find appalling," wrote Bloom. "What is astounding and degrading is the dogmatism with which we accept such relativism, and our easygoing lack of concern about what that means to our lives."[48]

In order to take the essential questions seriously, Bloom insisted, we must be prepared to find that our culture's responses to them (or another culture's responses to them) are wrong. Universities should not just be places that produce government-funded research to advance the latest technologies, nor should they merely be places that protect endowment-funded research to critique the government's funding priorities. Universities, for Bloom, should be places where young people can pose questions that go beyond the immediately instrumental and get at the core issues of being human—questions that challenge our everyday practices and our deepest values so as to provoke us to explore who we are, and who we might become. "A liberal education means precisely helping students pose this question [*What is man?*] to themselves, to become aware that the answer is neither obvious nor simply unavailable, and that there is no serious life in which this question is not a continuous concern. . . . The liberally educated person is one who is able to resist the easy and preferred answers, not because he is obstinate but because he knows others worthy of consideration."[49] One of the reasons Bloom's book struck such a nerve with American educators and the general public was because he wanted his readers to consider answers that were hierarchical and antidemocratic. Since the general culture applauded (at least officially) egalitarianism and democracy, universities should be places where very different possibilities should thrive. His anger at academia grew out of his sense that the forces within the university that deemed themselves the most progressive were actually the most conventional because they operated in accord with the prejudices of modernity. Although the mainstream academic response to Bloom painted him as politically conservative, *The Closing of the American Mind* railed against the deep conformism of the university. He cherished the university as a place where one should be able to see alternatives to contemporary conventions, but he thought the academy had become instead the vehicle for bolstering our post-Enlightenment assumptions. The idea of progress and the historicism out of which it grew were themselves responses to essential tensions in the human condition that arose in particular times and places. Bloom thought that we were in the process of forgetting the very traditions that gave rise to our own relativism and contained alternatives to it. And we were proud of our blindness to these alternatives.

Bloom's attack on the university was responded to with breathtaking ferocity because of his Olympian tone, his delight in attacking anything that was deemed progressive, and because he took his own impressions as evidence enough for his polemics. David Rieff's review in the *Times Literary Supplement* might have been the most extreme in declaring that the book was one "decent people would be ashamed of having written," but the fact that Bloom had written an antidemocratic book that appealed to a mass audience aroused more than the usual antipathy.[50] Camille Paglia would later note that *The Closing of the American Mind* was the first salvo in the culture wars, and the book would be followed by a wave of angry texts excoriating intellectuals, professors, students, or simply the young. For some, the issue was the abandonment of the Great Books; for others, it was caving into the "others" of Western culture; and for some of the shrillest commentators, the issue was "tenured radicals" bent on indoctrinating the young into their own secular, anti-Christian ways. These were all attacks on the university's failure to provide a common intellectual experience to undergraduates that would perpetuate some continuity with what previous generations regarded as essential learning. Still others criticized the university either for continuing traditions of prejudice that marginalized underrepresented groups or for acquiescing to a corporate culture that wanted to use the campus only as a tool for grooming managers.

In the 1980s and 1990s the culture wars were raging, and higher education was a primary battleground. What would be taught and to whom? We should remember Harvard president Eliot's faith that liberal education would evolve to expand the circle of teaching and learning as the results of the specialized postgraduate divisions of the university trickled down to the college level. However, since the number of courses that undergraduates took remained roughly the same, as new classes were added, others would have to go. Each subject area that fell out of favor had its supporters who just could not believe that someone "could graduate from this university without knowing X!" Just as in the nineteenth century protesting Princetonians were aghast that not everyone would learn Latin and Greek, in the late twentieth shocked Stanfordians were aghast that graduates of the highly selective university would never have encountered Homer and Shakespeare. Part of the reason for this, as W. B. Carnochan has noted, was a change in the notion of culture itself.[51] Whereas generations of students and professors had drawn on the Arnoldian conception of culture as a substitute for religion—the source of our nobility and our path to the highest things—by the late twentieth century an anthropological view of culture was ascendant. This meant that instead of seeing culture as the realm of lofty thoughts and sublime art, one saw culture as the common practices of a people that bound them together in daily life. In other words, the anthropological view made no distinction between culture and convention. And it makes no sense to pick out the "Great Conventions" for ennobling study. The anthropological view of culture as common practices was leveling and had a certain democratic appeal because it eschewed questions of value, let alone greatness. But if the study of culture wasn't ennobling, then why pursue it? The study of culture had been part of a rhetorical tradition of education that emphasized reverence for great works.[52] Without the lofty ambition of better understanding enduring questions that framed the human context, what was the goal of broad learning? Would exposure to diverse conventions followed in different parts of the world generate a sense of commonality? Without a shared sense of educational purpose, even within higher education itself, vocationalism appeared stronger than ever. If education is simply learning conventions of behavior, why not just learn the ones that will help you get ahead?

Throughout the twentieth century we have seen efforts to recalibrate what undergraduates should learn so that they would be prepared for professional work in or outside of the academy. A truly liberal education would be the base upon which further specialization could be built, or a foundation that would allow for a lifetime of learning and a deepening of experience. Over the last several years, however, we have seen a new sort of criticism directed at the academy. These contemporary critics no longer claim to be in search of "true liberal learning," but instead they call for an education that simply equips people to play an appropriate role in the economy. Education, from this perspective, is something you purchase; it should be thought of either as an investment or as an "experience" you pay someone else to provide you.

The current economic downturn, with its persistently high unemployment, is focusing more scrutiny than ever on "whether college is worth it." The steep increases in the cost of higher education over the last twenty-five years and the higher levels of debt for students whose job prospects are dim have drawn more and more attention to what many are calling "the higher-education bubble." The education sector is being scrutinized for its inefficiencies, its curious pricing and marketing strategies, and its tendency to generate infrastructure and operating costs for areas that seem tangential to instruction and research. How are schools responding to what students and families say they want from a "college experience," and how are these responses (and the demands) contributing to rising costs? Are students who enroll in colleges and universities graduating in a timely way and, if they do graduate, do we have a sense of what they've learned? These (and many more) questions are being asked with increasing urgency as families try to determine if undergraduates are getting the "return on investment" that they should from their bachelor's degrees.

These questions have come up in various forms for generations, and in the past they have been posed in order to steer schools toward providing the *real* liberal education we want from college. In other words, in the past critics have aimed to expand the realm of what counts as a liberal education. In recent years, however, critics have gone a step further (or is it back?) in arguing that some people just don't need the broad education promised by colleges because these folks will not be in jobs that will use advanced skills. Richard Vedder, director at the Center for College Affordability and Productivity, puts it this way. "The biggest problem is that we are turning out vastly more college graduates than there are jobs in the relatively high-paying managerial, technical and professional occupations to which most college graduates traditionally have gravitated. Do you really need a chemistry degree to make a good martini? Roughly one of three college graduates is in jobs the Labor Department says require less than a bachelor's degree."[53] Vedder believes in the "discipline of markets," and he thinks that if college graduates continue to find themselves in jobs for which the education is irrelevant, then families in the future will decide that college is just not worth the cost.

The bartender with a chemistry degree is the contemporary version of the farmer who reads the classics with pleasure and insight, or of the industrial worker who can quote Shakespeare. Where once these "incongruities" might have been hailed as signs of a healthy republic, today they are more likely to be cited as examples of a "wasted"—nonmonetized—education. To be sure, throughout our history America has produced minor writers and pundits of the moment who wonder why one would learn things that cannot be put to use on the job. To be sure, current controversies are rooted in the high cost of colleges and in the fact that greater numbers of students are going into deeper debt to finance their education. Furthermore, if ever more people are encouraged to get a college degree, won't the degree be worth less? Who wants to be a part of a club with that many members? Peter Wood, president of the conservative National Association of Scholars, complains: "Too many students are going to college—too many for their own good, but also too many for the good of college itself. The institution has overextended itself and can no longer achieve its deeper purposes." For Wood, the "deeper purposes" should be grounded in "college curricula rooted in the civilization that has sustained the university for more than a millennium, respect for rigorous intellectual inquiry and genuine scholarship." These purposes are akin to the idea of liberal learning (roughly of the sort defended in the *Yale Report* of 1828), emphasizing "the defense of Western civilization as providing the best and most coherent structure for an undergraduate curriculum."[54] If colleges and universities try to be everything to everybody, if they take as their mission providing credentials to anyone with a high school diploma, they will have abandoned their deeper purposes while not actually preparing people efficiently for the world of work. Rather than promoting the ever-expanding circle of the liberal arts, Wood and the National Association of Scholars would have us return to a common core of Western Civilization—by which they seem to mean European and American preindustrial values. They also seem to be very comfortable with the kinds of inequality that were characteristic of those societies.

The United States now ranks tenth among industrialized nations in terms of the percentage of young people (aged twenty-five to thirty-four) with a college degree. For the older cohort (thirty-five to sixty-four), we rank second. The percentage of those with degrees for each group is roughly the same, around 39 percent. Clearly, other industrialized countries have become more successful in steering students toward postsecondary education. The Obama administration has focused resources on changing this trend in the United States, as has the Lumina Foundation, which has set a goal "to increase the percentage of Americans who hold high-quality degrees and credentials to 60 percent by 2025." Lumina's work provides an interesting example of how the meaning of a college education has changed in recent years. For this well-endowed foundation, "higher education is a prerequisite to success in a knowledge-based society and economy." Workforce development is at the core of the organization's efforts, but it does recognize that "as we attain the goal, we improve the economy, strengthen civic engagement and reduce the costs of crime, poverty and health care and, in short, improve the human condition."[55] This list of secondary benefits of a more educated citizenry is linked to economic concerns but is not limited to them. Civic engagement and improving the human condition echo some of the positive dimensions long associated with liberal education. Lumina is also dedicated to reducing the disparities of college access between minorities and white students, which in turn should have an impact on economic inequality. Reducing inequality has been a goal for champions of liberal education since Jefferson.

But Lumina's approach to postsecondary education is in one respect quite different from those we've looked at thus far. Rather than considering what students should be taught, the foundation is part of a broad national movement that focuses on what students actually learn. At prestigious colleges and universities, professors have concentrated on earning the freedom to teach what they want and, in the best of cases, on what courses students should take to complete a major. But even then, the major is usually conceived as a preparation for graduate school in the field—despite the fact that the vast majority of students will not pursue advanced work of this sort. Students, for their part, have focused on which classes have the best reputation, and on which majors (and minors and double majors) are most likely to bring them success after graduation. Sometimes faculty and undergraduates come together to support courses of study that reflect their particular identity groups and political values. These programs are almost never proposed as requirements for all, but once legitimized they add to the vast array of academic choices. So many options, it's hard to keep track. How are these choices among classes related to what students are expected to learn?

Lumina, with significant backing from philanthropic institutions and governmental agencies, is trying to change this helter-skelter model (in which the ambitions of faculty and students are jumbled, if not discordant) by measuring what is actually "value-added" in a postsecondary education. It's not enough to have an admissions process that chooses really smart students who take classes for four years and leave with a diploma indicating that they've spent a certain amount of time in classrooms with other really smart people. How can we tell if the students' work at an institution has added to their intellectual capacity? Measuring what students learn, the president of Lumina has emphasized, is "absolutely vital in ensuring the *relevance* and *value* of a college credential." The word *credential* is important in that sentence. Given the wide variety of options available to students with a high school diploma who want to continue their education, many now think it's a mistake to focus exclusively on bachelor degrees. After high school one might receive a certificate, a credential, or a "badge" (a micro-credential) in anything from automobile electronics to cosmetology, from software development to ethnomusicology. But what makes a credential a *college* credential? Over most of the last two hundred years, the addition of the word *college* has generally indicated that the recipient of the credential had completed studies that were "liberal" in the sense of not being merely instrumental — but also preparing the student for more learning (which may or may not be relevant to a specific job). Today, for many the word *college* has come to mean simply a form of instruction that comes after high school. Some cheer this as a realistic response to the needs of a workforce that requires specific forms of training. Others, like Peter Wood, Richard Vedder, and a veritable beehive of op-ed writers, criticize this emphasis on education as the natural next step after high school. They think it's unrealistic to expect a large percentage of our population to remain in school beyond age eighteen. College, they insist, is not for everybody, and making it for everybody dumbs it down so much that it loses its real value.

Even the Lumina Foundation doesn't insist college is for everybody, but the organization is dedicated to helping the United States to move from 39 percent to 60 percent of the population finishing some sort of postsecondary work. They see this goal as vocational and do so without apology. Jamie P. Merisotis, the foundation's president, cites time and again the work of Anthony Carnevale of Georgetown's Center on Education and the Workforce, who "has estimated that, by 2018, 63 percent of all jobs will require some form of postsecondary education or training. That's a huge increase since the mid-'70s, when less than 30 percent of jobs required anything beyond a high school education."[56] So when the critics complain that we are letting too many people into postsecondary programs and calling that a college education, Merisotis counters that our workforce will need *more* people with better skills in the future. We don't need more bartenders with chemistry degrees for our country to remain competitive, but we do need more people who understand how to apply scientific principles to the changing kinds of work they are asked to do over the course of their careers. When defenders of more traditional college programs complain that we are dumbing down the undergraduate experience by linking it to vocational concerns, Merisotis responds defiantly as follows: "We need to abandon our historic view in higher education that we don't train people for jobs. Of course we do. That doesn't mean it is the *only* thing we do, but to deny that job skills development is one of the key purposes of higher education is increasingly untenable. Education also must equip people with the skills they need to adapt in whatever way is necessary as their lives change, jobs evolve, and new opportunities arise."[57] This is very much in keeping with the goals of liberal education since the time of Franklin: equipping people with skills they will be able to adapt over time, "as their lives change."

The American Association of Colleges and Universities (AAC&U) has joined with Lumina in showing how the integration of specific skills into academic itineraries can be effective in work beyond the university. In a series of initiatives meant to show the importance of a college education for an educated citizenry, a vibrant economy, and a shared culture, AAC&U has been making the case for contemporary relevance of liberal education. It emphasizes how broad, integrative learning increases a sense of social

responsibility, and how "essential learning outcomes" prepare students for a global economy.[58] Lumina's and
AAC&U's embrace of the rhetoric of job training is supple-
mented by their efforts to ensure that college completion
isn't achieved just by making the degree less rigorous and
meaningful. Lumina developed a degree qualifications
profile as a "shared definition of quality," "a baseline set of
reference points for what students in any field should be
able to do in order to earn their degrees." There are five
"basic areas of learning" in which all students in postsecondary degree programs should make progress: broad, integrative knowledge; specialized knowledge; intellectual
skills; applied learning, and civic learning. Faculty at each
institution should determine the local criteria for success-
fully demonstrating that students have indeed made progress, and students should understand what the expectations
are for them in these regards as they make their way toward
a degree. This contemporary version of liberal learning
emphasizes the ability to pull different skills together in
project-oriented classes and the ability to translate what
one learns in the classroom to work off campus. Lumina's
and AAC&U's ultimate aim is to weave some of the traditional qualities associated with liberal education together
with the practical challenges with which graduates are
faced once they leave school.[59]

If these organizations are trying to retool liberal learning, the Thiel Foundation proposes to abandon it entirely.
This mode of education is seen as no longer appropriate
(at least for very talented students) given the rapid pace of

technological and economic change. Peter Thiel, who attended Stanford as an undergraduate and went on to law school there, is one of those arguing strenuously that we are in an education bubble. The price of a college degree keeps being inflated because of artificial supports (like guaranteed student loans) and because families are really making a choice about consumption when they believe they are making a choice about investment.[60] This last point is key because Thiel has recognized that many students actually choose to attend a university because of the experience it provides—not because it prepares them for the future. And that's perhaps too gentle a way to put it. He calls college a four-year party.[61] *That*, he wants families to recognize, is what they are paying for; they are not making an investment in the future of a student. "Like housing was, college is advertised as an investment for the future. But in most cases it's really just consumption, where college is just a four-year party, in the same way that buying a large house with a really big swimming pool, etc., is probably not an investment decision but a consumption decision."[62] Of course, Thiel is aware that college graduates make significantly more money over the course of their careers than those who don't pursue a degree after high school. But he (and many others have made this point) thinks this is because colleges choose talented people who are likely to succeed — not because the schools add value to the lives of those who attend. Of course, the only thing that matters in this college-as-investment paradigm is financial value. It's all about the money.

Thiel, however, does more than talk the talk. Having made some good investment decisions about buying things online (Paypal) and creating social networks (Facebook), he has the money to walk the walk. Thiel has created a high-profile fellowship that pays people to stop going to college. Twenty people under twenty years old are given $100,000 to "pursue innovative scientific and technical projects, learn entrepreneurship, and begin to build the innovative companies of tomorrow."[63] The eager participants are mentored by entrepreneurs, scientists, and "thought leaders." The program has been well choreographed to capture the attention of the media, framed as an innovative alternative to the staid, traditional atmosphere of the academy. This quotation from Thiel is from the foundation's press release: "Pundits and hand-wringers love to claim that universities are the only path to a successful life. In truth, an inquisitive mind, rigorously applied to a deep-rooted problem can change the world as readily as the plushest academic lab. . . . In 1665 when Cambridge University closed due to the plague, Isaac Newton used his time away to pursue self-directed learning and ended up inventing calculus. The drive to make a difference is what truly matters."[64] Self-direction, drive, and a willingness to take risks: these (plus access to Silicon Valley capital) are the ideal characteristics of the young person today. "The ideal candidate has ideas that simply cannot wait. She or he wants to change the world and has already started to do it in some fashion."[65] Education, for such people on a mission, would just be a distraction. "What we want to suggest is that there are some very smart and very talented people who don't need college."[66] Here we are a long way from discussions of heritage or experimentation or well-roundedness. The innovation that Thiel wants to foster requires intelligence, to be sure, but his image of success suggests someone who is obsessive rather than expansive, someone whose justifiable impatience requires specialized "mentoring" rather than liberal learning.

You'll remember that Alan Bloom's main point about higher education, often obscured by his ideological rants and pseudo-philosophical posturing, was that the academy had abandoned its responsibility to make judgments about what was worth studying and why. Into this vacuum rushed critics of all sorts. Some claim that college education must return to its roots, others that it must be expanded to certify learning in a modern democracy, and still others that it is increasingly irrelevant in a rapidly changing, technologically driven world. Whether we see the university today as heir to Eliot's expanding circle of electives, or McCosh's distribution requirement controls on choices of study, Bloom is right that most universities today don't seem capable of articulating what students should learn. This task should fall to the faculty, but professors are naturally drawn to the subjects they themselves were taught. Nor does their hyperspecialized professional training serve them well in thinking about the curriculum as a whole. University administrators, for their part, have many constituencies to please and are loath to enter the fray. In 1987 Bloom's critique of higher education was labeled conservative because of his various allegiances, but his accusations have recently been echoed by commentators coming from left of center. Louis Menand, for example, describes the difficulties in getting any agreement on what students ought to study, even though he reports that there has been a return to the idea of general education in the last decade.[67] "No one [at Harvard] thought that what students needed to know was self-evident," he writes, "but most professors felt that whatever it was, the college had an obligation to give it to them."[68] But what was it? In his recent *College: What It Was, Is and Should Be*, Columbia professor Andrew Delbanco laments that "very few colleges tell their students what to think. With equally rare exceptions, most are unwilling even to tell them what's worth thinking about."[69] The only thing that faculty, students, and administrators seem to be able to agree on is that a liberal education should not be vocational. As Menand quips, "Garbage is garbage, but the *history* of garbage is scholarship. Accounting is a trade, but the *history* of accounting is a subject of disinterested inquiry—a liberal art."[70]

In the face of increasing demands for vocational instruction, the thin reed of "antivocationalism" has become a tenuous way of defining what comprises a liberal education. But what other choices do its defenders have? If we can no longer claim that it is important to know any particular subject area, how do we defend a mode of education that has no immediate utilitarian benefits? Until fairly recently, one could still depend on the *prestige* of a liberal education, the allure of having gone to a highly selective school at which a sign of one's intelligence was that one didn't have to take *merely* vocational courses. But the appeal of prestige was bound to wane in a society less and less inclined to make distinctions between culture and convention, between high and low, between subjects worth studying because of their intrinsic worth and subjects worth studying because they were popular or because they would help one make more money. This is not just the result of the recent economic crisis; there was a powerful elevation of careerism among students during the most recent hot economic times as well. Victor Ferrall cites a 2007 study "reporting that 92 percent of college bound students felt preparing for a career was very important, and only 8 percent found the availability of liberal arts education essential in choosing a college."[71]

Over the course of this chapter, we have seen various controversies concerning the forms of liberal education that were popular at any one time. Benjamin Franklin lampooned the idle, privileged students at Harvard, but he wanted to create the conditions for truly liberal learning in Philadelphia — first with his study group and finally with the University of Pennsylvania. For Franklin, the awakening of curiosity, learning to learn, was at the core of liberal education. Education reformers in the middle of the nineteenth century sought to change the mix of subjects taught — away from the dead languages and ornamental memorization and toward a truly broad base of learning. These reformers wanted education to be connected to research, and they saw their work as practical without being narrowly vocational. When Du Bois criticized Washington, he was pointing to a liberal education that was tied to systematic inquiry whose breadth indicated an investment in learning for its own sake. Addams showed that learning for its own sake could lead one to engagement in the community. Liberal learning did not necessarily mean study disconnected from the real problems afflicting one's fellow citizens. And throughout the twentieth century we have seen efforts to make liberal learning relevant to economic, social, and political issues of the day. In the wake of World War II, a general education was thought to provide one with the basic intellectual tools to resist political indoctrination and to find success in a growing economy. Today the image of the heroic entrepreneur is someone who is ultra-focused on turning an idea into a start-up that will attract investors. Steve Jobs and Bill Gates, both of whom dropped out of college, are icons of American ingenuity. Despite what each has said about the importance of a broad learning across a variety of fields, what their admirers take away is "learn only what you need to know to monetize your idea." Education, from this perspective, prepares people to be either consumers or, if they are talented enough, innovators. It's all about bettering chances of success in the markets in which we will participate.

In this context, pontificating that the best education is nonvocational is really just a trite appeal to the tradition of the leisured gentleman whose status was linked to not having to use his education to earn a living. This wasn't enough for Benjamin Franklin, and it isn't enough for our students today. The traditions of liberal education in the United States are much more robust than mere antivocationalism. Today we must draw on those traditions to once again articulate what liberal education is and why it matters. That's the subject of our final chapter.

4.

Reshaping Ourselves and Our Societies

IN THE LAST chapter, we saw a continuum of controversies concerning liberal education. In the colonial period, Benjamin Franklin skewered learning that took pride in its freedom from labor (in its uselessness) as just a mask for snobbism—learning to exit a drawing room properly. He went on, though, to propose a compelling version of a broad education that was useful without being narrowly instrumental. Over the course of the 1800s, we saw battles between those who wanted to preserve what they thought of as the classical core of liberal education, learning to recite Latin and Greek, and those who wanted to move higher education in the direction of specialized research relevant to contemporary problems. The growth of the professionalized research university dominated the evolution of higher education in the twentieth century, so much so that the most prestigious institutions were increasingly isolated from the work of educating undergraduates. The "liberal arts" and "general education" remained contentious topics in a country committed to technological change as an engine for economic development. Still, respect for forms of education not reducible to commerce was easy to find in popular culture even into the 1960s. A half century ago, Mike Nichols's film *The Graduate* satirized Benjamin's conversation with Mr. McGuire, who keeps repeating the word "plastics" to the young man. We knew we were supposed to laugh at the philistine adult. Despite some ambivalence, in those days educators and much of the public still expressed admiration for educated well-roundedness and critical thinking, even if it wasn't at all clear how exactly these were achieved.

Throughout the twentieth century, there has been a dramatic expansion of the numbers of people seeking some sort of college degree. In recent years, critics have been asking why so many people bother to pursue their education beyond high school. These radical instrumentalists question whether people destined to have low-paying jobs should be studying literature and history, on the one hand and, on the other, they ask why young entrepreneurs need to know anything beyond how to monetize their Web-based ideas. In the eyes of these critics, we in education are all traders either selling or buying playlists of things we know or want to know. Why should I bother to learn history, biology, or political science, when what I really want is a credential to get a better job in a large organization? Through "disruptive innovation," we are told, liberal learning can be "disintermediated" as we are encouraged to get to the point—a market transaction, the data traces of which will be used to encourage a new set of market transactions. Today, Mr. McGuire would whisper, "Digital media" or "Apps" to a young graduate. But would audiences still perceive a satire?

Although buzzwords like dis-intermediation, disruptive innovation, and playlist are fairly new, the pressure for a more narrowly tailored education, especially for those with limited economic prospects, is not. In 1906, for example, the Massachusetts Commission on Industrial and Technical Education developed a plan for a dual system of high school education wherein some students would be trained for specific kinds of jobs in the expanding industrial sector, while others would receive a broad education that would allow them to continue their studies in college. Over the next decade a wide range of interest groups ranging from the chamber of commerce to the American Federation of Labor came out in support of a national effort to stimulate vocational education. One of the most vocal opponents of this effort was a philosopher not at all unfriendly to the idea of integrating manual training into schools' curricula. John Dewey opposed the dual-track educational policy because he recognized that this approach was meant to reinforce existing unequal social relations. Those deemed unfit for broader forms of learning would be slotted into classes that taught them only how to perform a task currently demanded by industry. It wasn't that Dewey thought we should cultivate solely those facets of people unrelated to their working lives. He recognized that almost all Americans would have to find gainful employment and that education should prepare us for our occupations: "The world in which most of us live is a world in which everyone has a calling and occupation, something to do. Some are managers and others are subordinates. But the great thing for one as for the other is that each shall have had the education which enables him to see within his daily work all there is in it of large and human significance."[1] Education should aim at enhancing our capacities for finding "large and human significance" in what we do so that we would not be reduced to mere tools of an industrial system. "The kind of vocational education in which I am interested is not one which will adapt workers to the existing industrial regime; I am not sufficiently in love with the regime for that."[2]

John Dewey was the most significant American philosopher in the twentieth century to turn his attention to education. Although he lived in a very different historical context than our own, and although his focus was on the K-12 years, the space he carved out for liberal learning remains of vital interest for higher education today. Dewey rejected the modern forms of narrow vocationalism for the same reasons he rejected the traditional concentration on the Great Books: they were antidemocratic, and they set artificial boundaries on inquiry. His thinking about education and experience drew on Jefferson's pioneering pedagogical experiments, and Dewey reinvigorated the development of a broad, reflexive, and pragmatic version of liberal learning.

Dewey, a native of Burlington, Vermont, was born on the eve of the Civil War and died as the Korean War was getting under way. Intellectually, he came of age in the newly emergent research university, getting his doctorate in philosophy from Johns Hopkins University. He taught at the University of Michigan before accepting a professorship at the University of Chicago in 1894. Almost a decade later, after a dispute with Chicago's president William Rainey Harper over control of the lab school, Dewey moved to Columbia University, where he would spend the remainder of his exceptionally long career. Dewey's output was immense—the "later works" alone take up seventeen volumes. In these pages, I will focus on just a few of the philosopher's key ideas that are of especial relevance for rethinking liberal learning today.

Since the eighteenth century, education has been viewed in terms of the development of autonomy. As we learn, we become more capable of making our own decisions, less likely to suffer from dependence on those with authority. This was key to Jefferson's sense of the citizen as self-sufficient, as it was to Emerson's notion of self-reliance through self-transformation. A broader education, these thinkers argued, enabled us to have a deeper independence. Dewey's emphasis on the social dimensions of education was far stronger than either Jefferson's or Emerson's. Jane Addams had a powerful impact on Dewey's thinking after he moved to Chicago, especially in regard to the deep bond between ideas and action, theory and practice. People didn't work things out in their own heads and then find out if their mode of thinking might apply to the world. People learned by trying out new things, often in groups, and then revising and trying again. This process of experimentation was not focused on the individual; it was a social enterprise. As early as 1897, Dewey emphasized that the teacher's task was "not simply the training of individuals but the formation of the proper social life" (454). One didn't just achieve self-reliance through education, one participated in the "social consciousness of the race" (443) by using ideas in actions that mattered out in the world.

In *Democracy and Education* (1916) Dewey challenges the Enlightenment notion of autonomy head on: "From a social standpoint, dependence denotes a power rather than a weakness; it involves interdependence. There is always a danger that increased personal independence will decrease the social capacity of an individual. In making him more self-reliant, it may make him more self-sufficient; it may lead to aloofness and indifference. It often makes an individual so insensitive in his relations to others as to develop an illusion of being really able to stand and act alone—an unnamed form of insanity which is responsible for a large part of the remediable suffering of the world" (486). From Dewey's perspective, education is only possible because young people are open to interdependence. This is not something one wants them to "grow out of," but something that education should cultivate. The interdependence of human beings is an advantage because it is linked to human "plasticity," by which he means "the ability to learn from experience; the power to retain from one experience something which is of avail in coping with the difficulties of a later situation" (487). In learning, we retain impressions of the world around us and retain our relationships with other people—that is, we develop habits that help us to navigate in the world. This learning is potent as long as we remain active in seeking new impressions and building on our existing relationships. If, however, we develop habits that just allow us to conform to the world around us, to fit into existing conditions, then we have learned to stop learning. Such a result would be antieducational: having lost our ability to change ourselves and our society, we would become merely more or less useful components of society's contemporary form. As long as the world around us didn't change much, we would be fine (being adept at conforming to the status quo). But for at least the last two hundred years, it's been clear that change in the world is accelerating. Conforming to the world at any one time isn't good enough.

Education, from the Deweyan perspective, has for its goal only more education—a greater ability to continue to learn in a context of interdependence. "The inclination to learn from life itself and to make the conditions of life such that all will learn in the process of living is the finest product of schooling" (493). Learning in the context of living means modifying one's behavior on the basis of experience; it means trying things out and revising one's attempts through collaboration. It's not that one "gets an education" in order to "do things in the world"; it's that doing things in the world and getting an education are part of the same process. One is not prior to the other. When we are urged to learn in order to do some one thing in particular (usually for somebody else), we are being urged to conform to somebody's notion of what our role in society (or in a classroom, or in a economy) ought to be. Conformity is the enemy of learning because in order to conform you restrict your capacity for experience; you constrict your plasticity.

Doubt is the antidote to conformity because doubt about the way things are (or are said to be) encourages inquiry. For Dewey, certainty is the enemy of inquiry—not its promise. We should expect that inquiry will lead to more questions, more experiments, more learning. With learning, there is always risk, and educators harness the energy of that risk for creative purposes. "Systematic advance in invention and discovery began," Dewey wrote, "when men recognized that they could utilize doubt for purposes of inquiry" (503). Doubt becomes creative when it is linked to a spirit of investigation, a desire to learn that itself sparks more inquiry and experimentation. Dewey's pragmatic understanding of education emphasizes its prospective character—it is completely oriented toward the future. Liberal education, as we have seen, has also been connected to the increased freedom and autonomy of the individual and to enhancing the capacity of people to engage in meaningful work. But liberal education has always included a strong historical function, giving students access to the great intellectual, artistic, and political achievements of the past. Does education's participation in tradition have any role in the pragmatist's approach to learning?

Tradition does have an important role in Dewey's thinking about education insofar as the past is the basis for present inquiry. We have a fuller sense of the problems before us when we understand how people in the past have dealt with the challenges of their own times. At early ages, he argued, children should be taught how to make meaning out of the various facts that they learn about the past. Facts become meaningful to children if they can relate them to present concerns. In later years, historical study becomes more sophisticated, and students learn the value of finding patterns within a multiplicity of data. But for Dewey, presentism prevails. We make sense of the past in order to better equip ourselves to deal with problems in the present. This problems-oriented approach aroused the ire of historians who were offended that Dewey did not seem to care about the past for its own sake. They were right about the philosopher, although they were confused in claiming that he was a complete relativist who thought that you could make whatever claims you wanted concerning the past as long as they served the present. In fact, Dewey just insisted that historical knowledge, like all knowledge, was contingent, subject to revision, and that it served our current interests and desires. You could make more or less reasonable claims about specific events in the past, but you should do so knowing that these claims would be revised as research continued. This wasn't a claim about the reality of the past; it was a claim about knowledge leading to more inquiry to pursue questions of genuine import. As Dewey put it in 1917: "Anticipation is therefore more primary than recollection; projection than summoning of the past; the prospective than the retrospective." History could be harnessed to inquiry for the sake of the future, but there was no question of grasping the past for its own sake: "Imaginative recovery of the bygone is indispensable to successful invasion of the future, but its status is that of an instrument. . . . To isolate the past, dwelling upon it for its own sake and giving it the eulogistic name of knowledge, is to substitute the reminiscence of old age for effective intelligence" (64–65). Effective intelligence, from this pragmatist's perspective, might incline us to try to understand the past in its own terms, but there is no escape from the fact that we make that attempt to serve present purposes.

Opponents of this pragmatist view have criticized both its lack of respect for history "as it really was" and its notion that education should produce a "successful invasion of the future." What are the ethics of colonizing the past, mining it only for our own purposes? Hasn't the effort to "invade the future" turned into what Horkheimer and Adorno called the "triumphant calamity" of technology and Enlightenment? Dewey rejected calls to treat the past with reverence as "chewing a historic cud long since re-duced to woody fiber," and he saw no viable alternative to philosophy's "bring[ing] to consciousness America's own needs and its own principle of successful action." In 1917 he wrote: "If changing conduct and expanding knowledge ever required a willingness to surrender not merely old solutions but old problems it is now" (59).

In the middle of the twentieth century, this pragmatic, presentistic approach actually reinvigorated historical study. Historians such as Charles Beard, Mary Beard, Merl Curti, and Richard Hofstadter found Dewey's views an antidote to what they saw as sterile antiquarianism within the historical profession.[3] Pragmatism insisted that we write an account of the past beginning from present concerns, that we tell the story of the past in order to pursue particular goals that we find relevant. Dewey didn't think this led to relativism but instead to an awareness of the context of inquiry. Historians formed communities of inquiry, raising questions and concerns to be addressed by research. History's real importance was that it helped us deal with matters of interest now.

But Dewey was a philosopher, not a historian, and he called for a reorientation of his discipline away from general problems of knowledge and toward human problems in "The Need for a Recovery of Philosophy" (1917). The essay is a pragmatist manifesto, urging us away from knowledge as a picture that corresponds with the world and toward inquiry as an activist enterprise motivated by social and personal concerns. The goal of our intellectual endeavors should not be to mirror reality accurately but "to free experience from routine and from caprice." He wrote that "unless professional philosophy can mobilize itself sufficiently to assist in this clarification and redirection of men's thoughts, it is likely to get more and more sidetracked from the main currents of contemporary life" (59). Dewey calls for a pragmatism that will be "empirically idealistic, proclaiming the essential connexion of intelligence with the unachieved future." Philosophy should leave behind the "industry of epistemology" because "there is no problem of knowledge in general." But there are real problems of doing and of suffering, and philosophy should become "an outlook upon future possibilities with reference to attaining the better and averting the worse" (88).

"Philosophy recovers itself," Dewey wrote, "when it ceases to be a device for dealing with the problems of philosophers and becomes a method, cultivated by philosophers, for dealing with the problems of men" (95). One can substitute "education" for "philosophy" and get a pretty good idea of his approach to liberal learning. Our education must address human problems but, as we saw above in his objections to merely technical training, we should not limit ourselves to solving only the most mechanical of dilemmas. By addressing the most serious human problems through education, we are open to what he called "transfiguration"; we are open to changing our lives and the world around us.

At the close of his essay, Dewey wrote: *"We pride ourselves upon a practical idealism, a lively and easily moved faith in possibilities as yet unrealized, in willingness to make sacrifice for their realization."* "Practical idealism" was a phrase used by a president of Bowdoin College in the early twentieth century, by Gandhi a generation later, and embraced today by my own university, Wesleyan. The phrase captures some of the tensions and aspirations of contemporary liberal education. But Dewey warns us not to get too comfortable with our highfalutin phrases: "All peoples at all times have been narrowly realistic in practice and have then employed idealization to cover up in sentiment and theory their brutalities." Dewey warns against falling prey to merely covering over our brutalities with ideals and sentiment. A liberal education should help us develop the intellectual and moral capacities to imagine a future that is worth striving for, and enhance our ability to create the tools for its realization. This would be, to echo Dewey on philosophy, a sufficiently large task.

Dewey's writings on education are mainly concerned with schools, not universities, but in 1944, he published a brief essay in which he emphasizes that no college disciplines are "inherently liberal."[4] One can teach subjects with the aim of liberating the students, or one can teach them mechanically simply to train them. Once we drop, as we must, the notion that some people should be educated for leisure and others for work (the notion on which the traditional view of the liberal arts was based), the question becomes only: How can we educate people so that they can continue to learn through inquiry in their private and public lives? The development of the capacity for inquiry isn't due to the inherent properties of a set of traditional disciplines. This capacity is fostered by connecting subjects to "their humane sources and inspiration." "The problem of securing to the liberal arts college its due function in democratic society is that of seeing to it that the technical subjects which are now socially necessary acquire a humane direction. There is nothing in them which is 'inherently' exclusive; but they cannot be liberating if they are cut off from their humane sources and inspiration. On the other hand, books which are cut off from vital relations with the needs and issues of contemporary life themselves become ultra-technical." Liberal learning liberates by connecting the understanding of context and inspiration with the "ability to appraise the needs and issues of the world in which we live" (393). Both liberal education and pedantry might be fueled by a desire to learn for its own sake, but only the former would connect that love of learning to the needs and issues of our time. Doing so would in turn stimulate further inquiry—a virtuous circle of learning.

Dewey was clearly the most important American public intellectual of his day. As Henry Steele Commager famously put it: "So faithfully did Dewey live up to his own philosophical creed that he became the guide, the mentor, and the conscience of the American people; it is scarcely an exaggeration to say that for a generation no major issue was clarified until Dewey had spoken." "By the time of his death in 1952," Kloppenberg notes, "it was not possible to study the history of modern American ideas without paying close attention to pragmatism."[5] But the philosopher's fall from this pinnacle of influence was swift. Professional philosophy, as it was defined in specialized research universities, had long been suspicious of Dewey. After World War II the field was becoming increasingly "analytic," emulating the sciences in a quest for precision and certainty. Logical positivism and the turn to precise parsing of language took little from Dewey; he seemed an amateur in comparison with the focused specialization prized by these analytic philosophers. His emphasis on experience as the core of education similarly was thought to lack rigor, and we see complaints about schools—from professors of education and parents—increasingly couched as criticisms of the Deweyite cult of progressive education. Furthermore, as establishment-oriented American intellectuals looked for a foundation from which to mount the cold war, the pragmatist's notion of open-ended inquiry seemed dangerously relativistic. Pragmatists didn't claim to know the

Truth, and so they didn't seem capable of recognizing the threatening Evil of Communism. On the other end of the political spectrum, radical critics of American culture and education saw Dewey as too celebratory of the possibilities of progress. By the 1960s, the pragmatist's apparent lack of interest in deep structures (whether social, economic, or linguistic) and the absence of apocalyptic or messianic rhetoric was a sign to the New Left that pragmatism wasn't radical enough. A philosophy interested in what William James had called the "cash value" of ideas seemed too invested in the status quo.

Many have by now written about the decline of pragmatism after Dewey's death and its recent resurgence both in philosophy departments and the wider culture. No matter who is telling the story, the key figure in that resurgence is Richard Rorty, who developed a powerful and original perspective on the history of philosophy in which pragmatism emerges as the hinge between philosophical and postphilosophical culture. By linking pragmatism to the widely discussed theorists of postmodernism, Rorty made American philosophy relevant far beyond the walls of analytically oriented departments. He argued that James and Dewey had early on developed a sophisticated antifoundationalism that was the best framework for understanding how we might shape our culture and society. His *Philosophy and the Mirror of Nature* (1979) offered a historical account of how the very idea of representation had led thinkers astray by suggesting to them that philosophy could become an arbiter of accuracy, methodology, or "realness." Which sentences are closer to reality? Which modes of thought are really scientific? Which beliefs are rational? Who really loves Truth? Rorty thought that all these questions grew out of a misunderstanding of language and thinking: namely, that some forms of language and some forms of thinking were more closely tied to the world than others. If this were the case, then we would need an intellectual discipline (like epistemology) to help us measure this closeness, or a philosophical specialist to determine who was working on something "really real." Analytic philosophy itself (especially as practiced by W. V. Quine, Wilfred Sellars, and Donald Davidson) helped one to see that these approaches were unhelpful. In the wake of that critique, Rorty embraced the conception of language as a tool (not a mirror), and he suggested that we consider how the tool worked in various contexts. Rather than think of sentences as being "closer" to real (that is, nonlinguistic) stuff, he urged us to think of language (like other human attributes) as being *caused* by real stuff, or as being a response to reality. If we could lose the picture of language as representation and think of it as a tool, then much of what had preoccupied philosophers would simply disappear.

Sometimes Rorty suggested that with the demise of epistemology, philosophy itself would disappear. No wonder his philosophical colleagues responded so vigorously! Rorty laconically admitted that the university would still need people who were good at interpreting old texts in the field, just as it needed literature professors who were good at talking about the nineteenth-century novel in England or medieval poetry in France. But many philosophers thought they were doing more than finding new ways to talk about old texts. They thought they were solving problems and making progress. Rorty pointed out that the so-called problems that preoccupied philosophers in universities had become of no interest to anyone in the wider culture, and that the discipline-focused philosopher's notion of progress was akin to a scholastic thinker claiming that now he really knew how many angels fit on the head of a pin. Increasingly technical analytic philosophy was pretty useless; it made no difference to anybody else in the university (or the wider culture) what went on in the philosophy department. That's why Rorty started to talk about philosophy as cultural politics. He wanted to change the conversation and develop a kind of philosophy that would offer something of import to the wider culture. If it couldn't solve problems, at least it could tell stories that, as Dewey put it, "modify our sense of who we are."

Rorty's views on education grew out of his critique of philosophy and his conviction that learning can be enlivened once you give up on the idea of Truth as the mirror of nature. One shouldn't be looking for a form of learning that is closer to human nature; one should develop education as an instigation to inquiries that might help one get along in the world. He conceded that primary and secondary education is mostly about socialization, about "getting the students to take over the moral and political common sense of the society as it is." In this regard, his views overlap with those of E. D. Hirsch, whose calls for enhanced "cultural literacy" in elementary and high school education have been stirring up controversy for decades. Some see the lists of historical and literary references that Hirsch wants students to recognize as an invitation to the mind-numbing standardized testing that has plagued our schools in recent years. But in fact Hirsch has been a critic of such testing, and he has emphasized the importance of narrative competence for young students. The facts—his lists—come alive when they are embedded in compelling stories. As he and others have pointed out, instead of giving students the opportunity to have strong emotional and cognitive encounters with well-told narratives, we have drilled them into thinking that effective reading is a technique with measurable outcomes to be evaluated on standardized tests.

The antidote to rote learning and narrow skill building is the cultivation of curiosity through active learning. Another philosopher in the Deweyan tradition, Martha Nussbaum, has been an ardent champion for liberal learning at all levels of education. For Nussbaum this means a reflexive, Socratic pedagogy emphasizing the critical examination of oneself and what is taken for granted in the opinions of others. Hirsch opts for a more direct approach in identifying the knowledge base all citizens should have: "Giving everybody more knowledge makes everybody more competent, and creates a more just society. Since knowledge is the great equalizer, the schools have a huge opportunity and responsibility to provide more equal life chances for all students, no matter where they come from."[6]

Nussbaum's orientation is toward process rather than content, following Dewey, who emphasized "children's own activity as the source of their learning."[7] Education creates autonomy, thus preparing citizens for political participation. This means learning to abandon passivity, and Nussbaum quotes Dewey about changing from a position of "inert recipiency and restraint to one of buoyant outgoing energy."[8] Hirsch is at the other end of the educational reform spectrum. He doesn't want to depend on the buoyant energy of children to dictate what the curriculum should look like; he wants us to reach some consensus on what we think is important for our compatriots to know. In this regard, Hirsch is close to Rorty in their views of the socialization function of early education.

Although Rorty, Nussbaum, and Hirsch have different views of what constitutes liberal learning, they agree that such an education is crucial if we are to have a polity of active citizens rather than passive subjects. The goal, both reflexive and pragmatic, is for students to become independent, autonomous thinkers whose independence and autonomy are enhanced, not compromised, by interaction with others. Kant's notion of enlightenment as "emergence from self-imposed immaturity" suits their views very well, though they would probably prefer Dewey's identification of inquiry with hope, of cooperative learning with freedom. Education should prepare students to become citizens capable of civil disagreement. On the one hand, this view seems like common sense, but these days it also seems utopian given what passes for discourse in our decidedly uncivil public sphere.

Rorty shared Nussbaum's view about the importance of liberal learning for the preparation of citizens, but he also had a romantic notion of the self-transformation that learning made possible. Rorty felt a strong affinity with the Dewey who predicted that Emerson would one day be regarded as the greatest American philosopher. This was the Emerson who wanted colleges to set hearts aflame and animate the world. The three agreed that learning at the college level shouldn't be about transferring knowledge but about encouraging inquiry, and inquiry is encouraged by practice, by getting into the work of research. For Rorty, in contrast with Nussbaum, this work didn't just build on the foundations set by "progressive" early education; it shook up those foundations. Inquiry is often fueled by doubts about the "moral and political common sense" that one had been socialized into as a child. "The point of non-vocational higher education is, instead," Rorty wrote," "to help students realize that they can reshape themselves—that they can rework the self-image foisted on them by their past, the self-image that makes them competent citizens, into a new self-image that they themselves have helped to create."[9]

To understand liberal education's capacity to help students reshape themselves requires us to go beyond what many in the humanities have come to view as the centrality of critical thinking. In the absence of a canon of texts or set of skills that we can agree all students should learn, many have turned to the notion of "critical thinking" as a way to describe the benefits of inquiry that doesn't aim at specialization. While the term *critical thinking* seems to have acquired its current meaning in the 1940s, it was not until the 1960s that it took off in education circles—with the publication of Robert Ennis's "A Concept of Critical Thinking" in the *Harvard Educational Review*.[10] Ennis was interested in how we teach the "correct assessment of statements," and he offered an analysis of twelve aspects of this process. Ennis and countless educational theorists who came after him have sung the praises of "critical thinking." There is now a Critical Thinking Foundation and an industry of consultants to help you enhance this capacity in your teachers, your students, or yourself.

Our best college students are really good at being critical. Many students today assume being smart *means* being critical. To be able to show that Hegelian concepts of narrative foreclosed the non-European, or that Judith Butler's stance on vulnerability contradicts her conception of performativity, or that a tenured professor had failed to account for his, her, or hir's own "privilege"—these are marks of sophistication, signs of one's ability to participate fully in the academic tribe. But this participation, being entirely negative, is not only seriously unsatisfying; it is ultimately counterproductive. And not only because those outside the tribe see these marks of sophistication as politically correct groupthink.

The skill at unmasking error, or simple intellectual one-upmanship, is not totally without value, but we should be wary of creating a class of self-satisfied debunkers—or, to use a currently fashionable word on campus, people who like to "trouble" ideas. In overdeveloping the capacity to show how texts, institutions, or people fail to accomplish what they set out to do, we may be depriving students of the capacity to learn as much as possible from what they study. In a humanities culture in which being smart often means being a critical unmasker, our students may become too good at showing how things *don't* make sense. That very skill may diminish their capacity to find or create meaning and direction in the books they read and the world in which they live. Once outside the university, our students continue to score points by displaying the critical prowess for which they were rewarded in school. They wind up contributing to a cultural climate that has little tolerance for finding or making meaning, whose intellectuals and cultural commentators delight in being able to show that somebody else *is not to be believed.*

This is not just a contemporary problem. Already in the eighteenth century there were complaints about an Enlightenment culture that prized only skepticism, and that was satisfied only with disbelief. Today, though, we have become skeptical even about skepticism. We no longer have the courage of our lack of conviction. Perhaps that's why we teach our students that it's cool to say that they are engaged in *troubling* an assumption or a belief. To declare that one wanted to *disprove* a view would show too much faith in the ability to tell truth from falsehood. And to declare that one was receptive to learning from someone else's view would show too much openness to being persuaded by an idea that might soon be deconstructed (or simply mocked).

In training our students in the techniques of critical thinking, we may be giving them reasons to remain *guarded*—which can translate into reasons *not* to learn. The confident refusal to be affected by those with whom we disagree seems to have infected much of our cultural life: from politics to the press, from siloed academic programs (no matter how "multidisciplinary") to warring public intellectuals. As teachers, however, we must find ways for our students to open themselves to the emotional and cognitive power of subjects that might initially rub them the wrong way, or just seem foreign. Critical thinking is sterile without the capacity for empathy and comprehension that stretches the self.

One of the crucial tasks of liberal education should be to help students cultivate the willingness and ability to learn from material they might otherwise reject or ignore. This material will often surprise students and sometimes upset them. Students seem to have learned that teaching-evaluation committees take seriously the criticism that "the professor, or the material, made me uncomfortable." This complaint is so toxic because being made uncomfortable may be a necessary component of a liberal education. Creating a culture that values the desire to learn from unexpected and uncomfortable sources as much as it values the critical faculties would be an important contribution to our academic and civic life.

But contemporary liberal education should do more than supplement critical thinking with empathy and a desire to understand others from their own points of view. We should also supplement our strong critical engagement with social and cultural norms by developing modes of teaching that allow our students to enter in the value-laden practices of a particular culture to understand better how these values are legitimated: how the values are *lived* as legitimate. Current thinking in the humanities is often strong at showing that values that are said to be shared are really imposed on more vulnerable members of a particular group. Current thinking in the humanities is also good at showing the contextualization of norms, whether the context is generated by an anthropological, historical, or formal disciplinary matrix. But in both of these cases we ask our students to develop a critical distance from the context or culture they are studying. We have been less interested in investigating with our students how we generate the values we believe in, or the norms according to which we go about our lives. In other words, we have been less interested in showing how we make a norm legitimate than in sharpening our tools for delegitimation. Pseudo-scientific "explanations" of moral choices have only encouraged the spectatorial view of culture. Fascination with the automatic—be it watching which parts of the brain light up during particular experiences or embracing affect theory's attempt to short-circuit the intentional—is no real substitute for understanding how norms are lived as legitimate.[11]

If we educators saw ourselves more often as explorers of the normative rather than as critics of normativity, we would have a better chance to reconnect our intellectual work to broader currents in public culture. This is what Dewey had in mind when he said that you get only "educational confusion" when universities fail to connect what they teach with "the dominant interests and activities of the great body of the American people."[12] This does not have to mean an acceptance of the status quo, but it does mean an effort to understand the practices of cultures (including our own) from the point of view of those participating in them. This would be to abandon what Rorty criticized as the "spectatorial" theoretical Left—the position that was good at unmasking but not at experimenting with new ways of living, including efforts to understand how cultures change. For many, this would mean complementing our literary or textual work with participation in community, with what are often called "service-learning" or "community-partnership" courses. For others, it would mean approaching our object of study not with the anticipated goal of exposing weakness or mystification but with the goal of turning ourselves in such a way as to see how what we study might inform our thinking and our lives.

Liberal education in America has always been comprised of the intertwined traditions of philosophy and rhetoric, of inquiry in pursuit of truth and performance in pursuit of excellence.[13] In the last half century, the liberating promise of inquiry has been dominant, but it has been inquiry often modeled on the detachment of objectivity. The inquirer has taken the guise of the sophisticated (often ironic) spectator rather than the messy participant in ongoing experiments or the reverent beholder of great cultural achievements. In the humanities in particular we need the energy of participation and the capacity to absorb ourselves in great works of literature, art, and science. Absorption is an endangered species of cultural life as technological surfing molds our receptive capacities. Of course critical reflection is fundamental to teaching and scholarship, but fetishizing detachment as a sign of intelligence has contributed to depleting our cultural resources. In pointing to the rhetorical tradition and the importance of absorption, I am underscoring a mode of liberal education that many practice already. It is a mode that can take language very seriously, but rather than seeing it as the master mediator between us and the world, a matrix of representations always doomed to fail, it sees language as itself a cultural practice to be understood from the points of views of its users. The fact that language fails according to some impossible criterion, or that we fail in our use of it, is no news, really. It is part of our finitude, but it should not be taken as the key marker of our humanity. The news that *is* brought by liberal learning is a way of turning the heart and the spirit so as to hear possibilities of various forms of life in which we might actively participate. When we learn to read or look or listen intensively, we are not just becoming adept at uncovering yet more examples of the duplicities of culture and society. We are partially overcoming our own blindness by trying to understand something from another's point of view. As William James said of this blindness: "The meanings are there for others, but they are not there for us."[14] For James, recognition of this blindness was key to education as well as the development of democracy and civil society. Of course hardnosed critical thinking may help in these endeavors, but it also may be a way we learn to protect ourselves from the acknowledgment and insight that liberal education have to offer. As students and as teachers we sometimes crave that protection because without it we risk being open to changing who we are. In order to overcome this blindness, we risk being very "uncomfortable" indeed.

Liberal education will continue to be a fundamental part of higher education if its scholarly habits of offering criticism are joined to making connections and finding ways to acknowledge practices that seem at first opaque or even invisible. This is a capacity for seeing possibilities, of detecting value that is fundamental for innovation as well as empathy. In supporting a rebalancing of critical thinking and practical exploration, I am echoing comments made by two of my own teachers, Louis Mink and Rorty. Mink was a philosopher of history deeply interested in how narrative can embody knowing. Years before Rorty deconstructed the idea of the "philosopher as referee," Mink suggested that critics "exchange the judge's wig for the guide's cap." I think we may say the same for teachers more generally, who can, in his words, "show us details and patterns and relations which we would not have seen or heard for ourselves." Learning to see and hear for oneself, acquiring the capacity to acknowledge meaning to which one had previ-

ously been blind, is one of the great gifts of liberal education. My professors enriched my life by showing me
"details and pattern and relations." I'd been deaf and blind
to many things around me, and I'd learned how to offer
criticisms that would allow me to avoid things and people
that were out of my comfort zone. My teachers helped me
to overcome some of this blindness, and this has allowed
me to have a greater variety and depth of experience than
I'd ever anticipated. In so doing they also helped me to acquire tools that have informed my work and my interac-
tions with colleagues and students. As guides, not judges,
we can show our students how to engage in the practice of
exploring objects, norms, and values that inform diverse
cultures. Through this engagement, students will develop
the ability to converse with others about shaping the objects, norms, and values that will inform their own lives.
They will develop the ability not merely to criticize values
but to add value to the organizations in which they participate. They will often reject roads that others have taken,
and they will sometimes chart new paths. But guided by a
liberal education they will increase their ability to find together ways of living that have meaning and direction. This
is why liberal education matters far beyond the university.

As I was finishing this book, I traveled to China to deliver
a lecture on liberal education at the Institute for Humanistic
Studies at Peking University. I didn't quite know what to
expect. It was intersession there, and I was told that there

might be a small group of about a dozen faculty and graduate students in attendance. In China there is increasing interest in liberal education, while here in the United States there is plenty of pressure on liberal learning from people who want our education system to have a more direct connection to jobs. These Americans seem to think that an education for "the whole person" is just too soft in this hypercompetitive, technology-driven age. These folks want a more routinized, efficient, and specialized education to train students for jobs. Yesterday's jobs, I tend to think.

In the States, I spend a fair amount of time arguing that this call for more efficient, specialized education is a self-defeating path to conformity and inflexibility—just the kinds of traits that will doom one to irrelevance in contemporary culture and society. How would this message resonate in China, which has had an educational system that is even more test-driven and hyperspecialized? I decided to take a historical approach, using my work on this book to show how our modern notions of liberal learning emerge from the intellectual history of the United States since its founding. Perhaps I would learn in the discussions after the talk about elements from Chinese traditions that would resonate with our history and that would have lessons for our contemporary situation.

Imagine my surprise when I entered a packed lecture hall. There were more than two hundred faculty and students present, despite the school vacation. My translator, the excellent Liu Boyun, was ready to leap in every few sentences, no mean feat, since I was speaking extemporaneously about a series of thinkers from Thomas Jefferson to Richard Rorty! I structured the talk using the concepts Liberate, Animate, Cooperate, Instigate/Innovate. Of course, they don't rhyme in Chinese . . .

With "Liberate," I talked about Jefferson and his belief that education would liberate us from what Kant had called "self-imposed immaturity." Jefferson, as you'll remember, was determined that students not have to choose their specific course of learning at the very start of their studies. You should discover what you are going to do through education — not sign up to be *trained* in a vocation before you know who you might be and what you might be able to accomplish. Sure, there would be mistakes, false roads taken. But, as Jefferson wrote to Adams, "Ours will be the follies of enthusiasm," and not of bigotry.

I pointed out, following the powerful writings of David Walker and Frederick Douglass, the enormous inconsistency in Jefferson's thinking. Here was a slaveholder who tied education to liberation. He was a determined racist who wrote of the importance of allowing young people to fail as they found their enthusiasms — obviously, only some people. Having good ideas about education doesn't make one immune to scandalous hypocrisy.

With "Animate," I turned to Ralph Waldo Emerson's hope that education would set souls aflame. Emerson saw routinized education as a form of corruption, and he urged his auditors to throw off the shackles of imitation that had become so prominent in colleges and universities. Colleges serve us, he wrote, when they aim not to drill students in rote learning but to help them tap into their creativity so that they can animate their world. I sensed a strong positive response to this from the audience, many of whom want to move away from the regime of test taking that structures Chinese secondary education (and is increasingly prominent in the United States). But what did they think of another of Emerson's ideas I talked about, that of "aversive thinking," the kind of thinking that cuts against the grain of authority?

With "Cooperate" I talked about thinkers associated with pragmatism: James, Addams, Du Bois, and Dewey. From James I emphasized the notion that "the whole function of thinking is but one step in the production of habits of action." Liberal education isn't about studying things that have no immediate use. It is about creating habits of action that grow out of a spirit of broad inquiry. I also talked about his notion of "overcoming blindness" by trying to put oneself in someone else's shoes. Seeing the world from someone else's perspective without leaping to judgment was fundamental for James.

As you'll recall, that notion of overcoming blindness toward others was also key for Jane Addams, whose idea of "affectionate interpretation" I stressed under the "Cooperate" rubric. Addams allows us to see how "critical thinking" can be overrated in discussions of liberal education. We need to learn how to find what makes things work well and not just how to point out that they don't live up to expectations. For Addams, compassion, memory, and fidelity should be linked together with understanding within a context of community. That context was also of decisive importance for Du Bois, who thought of education as a form of empowerment—but not just individual empowerment. For him, liberal learning enhanced the ability to "understand whither civilization is tending and what it means." This ability to grasp the meaning and direction of change benefited entire communities. These notions clearly resonated with the audience, and it was pointed out to me that Addams's and Du Bois' thinking had strong affinities with Confucian traditions.

My last thinker within the "Cooperate" rubric was John Dewey, and I cited his notion that philosophy "recovers itself . . . when it ceases to be a device for dealing with the problems of philosophers and becomes a method, cultivated by philosophers, for dealing with the problems of men." This is what pragmatic liberal education should do, too: take on the great questions of our time with the methods cultivated by rigorous scholarship and inquiry.

For Dewey, as we have seen in this chapter, no disciplines were intrinsically part of liberal education. The contextual and conceptual dimensions of robust inquiry made a subject (any subject) part of liberal learning. Furthermore, Dewey insisted that humanistic study would thrive only if it remained connected to "the interests and activities" of society. The university should not be a cloister; it should be a laboratory that creates habits of action through inquiry laced with compassion, memory, and fidelity.

I brought my talk to a close under the rubric "Instigate/ Innovate," referring to Rorty's view that liberal education at the university level should incite doubt and challenge the prevailing consensus. Aversive thinking that challenges the status quo, I stressed, is key to the power of liberal education today: instigating doubt that will in turn spur innovation. What we need is not just new apps to play with but new strategies for dealing with fundamental economic, ecological, and social problems. Only by creatively challenging the prevailing consensus do we have a chance of addressing these threats to our future.

I was surprised by the enthusiasm with which these remarks were greeted. I'd imagined, so wrongly, that talk about challenging the prevailing consensus would meet with a chilly reception at Peking University. On the contrary, the professors and students in the audience were looking to their own traditions and to those of the West for modes of aversive thinking that would empower them to meet the massive challenges facing their society. When I returned to the United States, I received an e-mail from seventy-five English majors at Inner Mongolia University who admonished me that liberal learning in China went back centuries, and that it "was never a disconnected or remote theory, never mere abstraction or mental exercise, but always had as its fundamental mission or *telos* the refinement of the student for the purpose of nurturing and guiding the nation as a whole." My new colleagues in China had high hopes for an evolving education system that would be less concerned with plugging people into existing niches and more concerned with teaching the "whole person" in ways that would liberate students' capacities for finding their own way while making a positive difference in the world. Free speech and free inquiry, from my perspective, will be crucial for that evolution. When will it be allowed to flourish?

My experience in China raises my own hope that the thoughtful inquiry sparked by liberal education will enable diverse communities to overcome more of their blindness to one another and to the problems they (and we) share. Will pragmatic liberal education instigate skillful and compassionate strategies for addressing our most pressing challenges? My brief visit suggests to me that it is more than a "folly of enthusiasm" to think that just maybe it will.

The mission of liberal learning in higher education should be to teach students to liberate, animate, cooperate, and instigate. Through doubt, imagination, and hard work, students come to understand that they really can reshape themselves and their societies. Liberal education matters because by challenging the forces of conformity it promises to be relevant to our professional, personal, and political lives. That relevance isn't just about landing one's first job; it emerges over the course of one's working life. The free inquiry and experimentation of a reflexive, pragmatic education help us to think for ourselves, take responsibility for our beliefs and actions, and become better acquainted with own desires, our own hopes. Liberal education matters far beyond the university because it increases our capacity to understand the world, contribute to it, and reshape ourselves. When it works, it never ends.

Notes

∎

INTRODUCTION

1. See, for example, Bruce Kimball, *Orators and Philosophers: A History of the Idea of Higher Education* (New York: Teachers College Press, 1986); *The Condition of American Liberal Education: Pragmatism and a Changing Tradition*, ed. Robert Orrill (New York: College Board, 1995); Francis Oakley, *Community of Learning: The American College and the Liberal Arts Tradition* (New York: Oxford University Press, 1992); W. B. Carnochan, *The Battleground of the Curriculum: Liberal Education and the American Experience* (Stanford: Stanford University Press, 1993); and Geoffrey Galt Harpham, *The Humanities and the Dream of America* (Chicago: University of Chicago Press, 2011).

2. The increasing interest in liberal education in China, Singapore, and Korea has been seen as a reaction against policies of rote learning that emphasize standardized testing and as tapping into Confucian notions of whole-person education. See, for example, the work of Tu Wei-Ming and Vera Schwarcz on ideas of Enlightenment in China. See also Daniel Bell's *China's New Confucianism: Politics and Everyday Life* (Princeton: Princeton University Press, 2010), chap. 7; Stephen Angle, *Sagehood: The Contemporary Significance of Neo-Confucian Philosophy* (Oxford: Oxford University Press, 2012), part 3.

3. See my "Beyond Critical Thinking," in *Memory, Trauma and History: Essays on Living with the Past* (New York: Columbia University Press, 2011), 234–38.

4. Thomas Jefferson to George Wythe, 1786, in *The Writings of Thomas Jefferson*, ed. Andrew Lipscomb and Albert Bergh (Washington, D.C.: 1903–4), 5:396.

5. Thomas Jefferson to George Ticknor, July 16, 1823, in *Writings*, 15:455.

6. Ralph Waldo Emerson, "The American Scholar," in *The Essential Writings of Ralph Waldo Emerson* (New York: Modern Library, 2000), 51.

7. John Dewey, *Democracy and Education: An Introduction to the Philosophy of Education* (New York: Macmillan, 1916), 360.

8. Richard Rorty, "Education as Socialization and as Individualization," in *Philosophy and Social Hope* (New York: Penguin, 1999), 118.

1.

FROM TAKING IN THE WORLD TO
TRANSFORMING THE SELF

1. Richard D. Brown, "Bulwark of Revolutionary Liberty: Thomas Jefferson's and John Adams's Programs for an Informed Citizenry," in *Thomas Jefferson and the Education of a Citizen*, ed. James Gilreath (Washington, D.C.: Library of Congress, 1999), 93.

2. Douglas L. Wilson, "Jefferson and Literacy," in Gilreath, 80.

3. Lorraine Smith Pangle and Thomas L. Pangle, *The Learning of Liberty: The Educational Ideas of the American Founders* (Lawrence: University of Kansas Press, 1993), 4.

4. Letter to Thaddeus Kosciusko (1810), quoted in ibid., 108.

5. Gordon Lee, "Learning and Liberty: The Jeffersonian Tradition," in *Crusade against Ignorance: Thomas Jefferson on Education*, ed. Gordon Lee (New York: Teachers College Press, 1961), 19.

6. From the bill *On the More General Diffusion of Knowledge*, quoted by Jennings L. Wagoner Jr., " 'That Knowledge Most Useful to Us': Thomas Jefferson's Concept of Utility in the Education of Republican Citizens," in Gilreath, 120.

7. Pangle and Pangle, 96.

8. Brown, 96.

9. *Report of the Commissioners for the University of Virginia (1818)*, quoted in Lee, *Crusade against Ignorance*, 118.

10. Benjamin Rush, "Address to the People of the United States," quoted in Pangle and Pangle, 148.

11. Washington, Eighth Annual Message, December 7, 1796, quoted in Pangle and Pangle, 150–52. See also David L. Madsen, *The National University: Enduring Dream of the USA* (Detroit: Wayne State University Press, 1966).

12. The Pangles point out (148) that Rush himself had grave doubts about the corrosive effects of learning without the influence of religion. This from a letter to a future trustee of Dickinson College, the Presbyterian school he founded: "Religion is necessary to correct the effects of learning. Without religion, I believe, learning does real mischief to the morals and principles of mankind."

13. See Jon Meacham's account of the Rockfish Gap meeting in *Thomas Jefferson: The Art of Power* (New York: Random House, 2012), 467–70. Jefferson himself was aware that his association with the university project also created impediments for its success. "Would it promote the success of the institution most for me to be in or out of it? Out of it, I believe. . . . There are fanatics both in religion and politics, who, without knowing me personally, have long been taught to consider me as a raw head and bloody bones" (letter to Joseph C. Cabell, February 26, 1818, quoted in Jennings L. Wagoner Jr., *Jefferson and Education* [Charlottesville: University of Virginia Press, 2004], 114).

14. Rockfish Report, in Lee, *Crusade against Ignorance*, 119.

15. "The rock which I most dread is the discipline of the institution, and it is that on which most of our public schools labor. The insubordination of our youth is now the greatest obstacle to their education. We may lessen the difficulty, perhaps, by avoiding too much government, by requiring no useless observances, none which shall merely multiply occasions for dissatisfaction, disobedience and revolt by referring to the more discreet of themselves the minor discipline, the graver to the civil magistrates." Jefferson to Ticknor, July 16, 1823, 15:455.

16. "A mind employed is always happy. This is the true secret, the grand recipe for felicity." Jefferson to his daughter Martha, May 21, 1787, quoted in Wagoner, " 'That Knowledge Most Useful,' " 125.

Wagoner notes that although Jefferson has no extensive plans for the education of women, he thought that republican women should have instruction that would allow for the "pursuit of happiness in the broadest sense."

17. Ibid.

18. Jefferson to Nathaniel Macon, January 12, 1819, quoted in Pangle and Pangle, 178.

19. Pangle and Pangle, 166.

20. Ibid., 167.

21. See Wagoner, " 'That Knowledge Most Useful.' "

22. Jefferson to Ticknor, July 16, 1823.

23. Wagoner, " 'That Knowledge Most Useful,' " 123.

24. See Pangle and Pangle, 102–5.

25. Wagoner, " 'That Knowledge Most Useful,' " 125.

26. See Jefferson's letter to the Marquis de Chastellux, June 7, 1785, quoted in Donald A. Grinde Jr., "Thomas Jefferson's Dualistic Perceptions of Native Americans," in Gilreath, 195.

27. C. Vann Woodward, "The Old and New Worlds: Summary and Comment," in Gilreath, 209–17. See also Grinde in the same volume.

28. Thomas Jefferson, *Notes on the State of Virginia*, query 18, http://xroads.virginia.edu/~hyper/jefferson/ch18.html (accessed July 2013).

29. Ibid., query 14, http://xroads.virginia.edu/~hyper/jefferson/ch14.html.

30. Ibid.

31. Ibid., query 18.

32. Ibid.

33. Ibid.

34. *Walker's Appeal, in Four Articles; Together with a Preamble, to the Coloured Citizens of the World, but in Particular, and Very Expressly, to Those of the United States of America, Written in Boston, State of Massachusetts, September 28, 1829*, 32, http://docsouth.unc.edu/nc/walker/walker.html (accessed June 2013). Subsequent references to this work are given parenthetically in the text.

35. See Howard Zinn and Anthony Arnove, *Voices of a People's History of the United States* (New York: Seven Stories, 2004), 168.

36. Frederick Douglass, *Narrative of the Life of Frederick Douglass*, chap. 6, http://classiclit.about.com/library/bl-etexts/fdouglass/bl-fdoug-narrative-6.htm (accessed June 2013). Subsequent references to this work are given parenthetically in the text.

37. Frederick Douglass, *Oration, Delivered in Corinthian Hall, Rochester, by Frederick Douglass, July 5th, 1852*, http://www.lib.rochester.edu/index.cfm?page=2945 (accessed June 2013).

38. Ralph Waldo Emerson, *Selected Writings of Emerson*, ed. Donald McQuade (New York: Modern Library, 1981), xii. See Emerson's journal entry, June 2, 1832, in *The Journals and Miscellaneous Notebooks of Ralph Waldo Emerson*, ed. W. H. Gilman et al., 14 vols. (Cambridge, Mass.: Harvard University Press, 1960–77).

39. Harold Bloom, "The Sage of Concord," *Guardian*, May 24, 2003, http://www.theguardian.com/books/2003/may/24/philosophy (accessed July 2013).

40. See Kenneth S. Sacks, *Understanding Emerson: "The American Scholar" and His Struggle for Self-Reliance* (Princeton: Princeton University Press, 2003), 10–15; quotation from 13.

41. Emerson, "The American Scholar," 45. Subsequent references to this work are given parenthetically in the text.

42. See Sacks, 38. The internal quotation is from Quincy's son.

43. Ibid., 41.

44. Ibid.

45. Emerson, "Self-Reliance," in *Selected Writings*, 129. Subsequent references to this work are given parenthetically in the text.

2.

PRAGMATISM: FROM AUTONOMY TO RECOGNITION

1. Booker T. Washington, "Industrial Education for the Negro" (1903), http://www.teachingamericanhistory.org/library/index.asp?document=62 (accessed July 2013).

2. Quoted on the website of Hampton University at http://www.hamptonu.edu/about/history.cfm (accessed July 2013).

3. W. E. B. Du Bois, *The Souls of Black Folk* (New York: Tribeca Books, 2013), 19. Subsequent references to this work are given parenthetically in the text.

4. Booker T. Washington, "Industrial Education for the Negro," in *The Booker T. Washington Reader* (Radford, Va.: Wilder), 357.

5. Quotations from "The Talented Tenth," http://www.yale.edu/glc/archive/1148.htm (accessed June 2013).

6. Ibid. (about a third through the essay).

7. For a thoughtful consideration of this influence, see Robert Gooding-Williams, *In the Shadow of Du Bois: Afro-Modern Political Thought in America* (Cambridge, Mass.: Harvard University Press, 2009). On the debate between Washington and Du Bois, see 90–94. See also the biographies of Du Bois by David Levering Lewis, especially *W. E. B. Du Bois: Biography of a Race, 1868–1919* (New York: Holt, 1994), 405–7.

8. "Talented Tenth," first paragraph.

9. Ibid.

10. Ibid., final sentences.

11. See Louis Menand, *The Marketplace of Ideas: Reform and Resistance in the American University* (New York: Norton, 2010), 44.

12. Ibid., 49, quoting Eliot in the *Atlantic Monthly*. See also Andrew Delbanco, *College: What It Was, Is and Should Be* (Princeton: Princeton University Press, 2012), 83–85.

13. Du Bois' autobiography, quoted by Sieglinde Lemke, "Berlin and Boundaries: *Sollen* versus *Geschehen*," *boundary 2* 27, no. 3 (2000): 51.

14. Gustav Schmoller was of crucial importance to Du Bois as he exemplified the possibility of the activist academic. Kenneth D. Barkin, " 'Berlin Days,' 1892–1894: W. E. B. Du Bois and German Political Economy," *boundary 2* 27, no. 3 (2000): 79–101.

15. Ibid., quoting W. E. B. Du Bois, "My Evolving Program for Negro Freedom," in *What the Negro Wants*. This is the epigraph for Barkin's article.

16. W. E. B. DuBois, *The Education of Black People: Ten Critiques, 1906–1960*, ed. Herbert Aptheker (Amherst: University of Massachusetts Press, 1973), 12.

17. Ibid., 14–15.

18. Ibid.

19. See Louise W. Knight, *Jane Addams: Spirit in Action* (New York: Norton, 2010), 41: "This is how culture persuades a strong mind to give up its efforts to think for itself."

20. Jean Bethke Elshtain, "A Return to Hull-House: Taking the Measure of an Extraordinary Life," in *The Jane Addams Reader*, ed. Jean Bethke Elshtain (New York: Basic, 2002), xxiv.

21. Ibid., xxv.

22. Jane Addams, "The Snare of Preparation," in *Jane Addams Reader*, 103–4.

23. Jane Addams, "The Modern Lear," in *Jane Addams Reader*, 168.

24. See Victoria Bissell Brown, *The Education of Jane Addams* (Philadelphia: University of Pennsylvania Press, 2004), 287–92.

25. Addams, "The Modern Lear," 176.

26. Quoted by Knight, 101.

27. See Elshtain.

28. See my "Why We Value Diversity," *Huffington Post*, February 23, 2012, http://www.huffingtonpost.com/michael-roth/why-we-value-diversity_b_1297938.html (accessed July 2013).

29. Apparently James steered Du Bois away from the path of teaching philosophy because it was so hard to earn a living in this field.

30. Quoted in Knight, 142.

31. Louis Menand, *The Metaphysical Club* (New York: Farrar, Straus and Giroux, 2001), 77. The quote from James is from Bernard Berenson's diaries.

32. See ibid., 219–20.

33. See *The Writings of William James: A Comprehensive Edition*, ed. John J. McDermott (Chicago: University of Chicago Press, 1977), 629–45. Subsequent references to this work are given parenthetically in the text.

3.

CONTROVERSIES AND CRITICS

1. Silence Dogood (Benjamin Franklin), *New England Courant*, May 14, 1722, http://www.ushistory.org/franklin/courant/silencedogood.htm (accessed July 2013).

2. Benjamin Franklin, *Autobiography*, chap. 5, http://www.let.rug.nl/usa/biographies/benjamin-franklin/chapter-5.php (accessed July 2013).

3. See Alan Houston, *Benjamin Franklin and the Politics of Improvement* (New Haven: Yale University Press, 2010), 80.

4. See Barnard Bailyn, as quoted in ibid., 80–81.

5. See Lorraine Smith Pangle, *Political Philosophy of Benjamin Franklin* (Baltimore: Johns Hopkins University Press, 2007), 105–12.

6. See Merle Curti, *The Social Ideas of American Educators* (Totowa, N.J.: Littlefield, Adams, 1968), 35–40.

7. Quotations in this paragraph drawn from Franklin, *Proposals Relating to the Education of Youth in Pensilvania* (Philadelphia, 1749), http://www.archives.upenn.edu/primdocs/1749proposals.html (accessed June 2013).

8. Andrew Delbanco summarizes things this way: "No doubt some antebellum colleges were regressive, stuffy and mired in the past. Others were restless, open and vibrant. . . . Whatever their particular creed in what has been aptly called 'an age of moral pedagogy,' they agreed that their primary purpose remained the development of sound character in their students," *College*, 72–73.

9. John Henry Newman, *The Idea of a University* (New Haven: Yale University Press, 1996), 76.

10. Ibid., 77.

11. David Potts, *Liberal Education for a Land of Colleges: Yale's Reports of 1828* (New York: Palgrave Macmillan, 2010), 4.

12. *Life, Letters and Journals of George Ticknor*, ed. George Stillman Hillard (London: Sampson Low, Marston, Searle and Rivington, 1876), 357.

13. Ibid., 363.

14. Ibid., 356.

15. Ibid., 364. For a recent take on Ticknor, see Warner Berthoff's article in *Harvard Magazine*, January–February 2005, http://harvard-magazine.com/2005/01/george-ticknor.html (accessed June 2013).

16. The *Yale Reports* have recently been made available in a very helpful edition by David Potts: *Liberal Education for a Land of Colleges*. References to the reports are given parenthetically in the text.

17. See Potts's commentary on the reports.

18. Wilhlem von Humboldt, "On the Internal and External Organization of the Higher Scientific Institutions in Berlin," trans.

Thomas Dunlap, http://germanhistorydocs.ghi-dc.org/sub_document.cfm?document_id=3642 (accessed July 2013).

19. Charles Eliot, "The New Education," *Atlantic Monthly*, February 27, 1869, http://www.theatlantic.com/magazine/archive/1869/02/the-new-education/309049/ (accessed June 2013). Subsequent quotations from Eliot in this paragraph and the next are from the same source.

20. Daniel Gilman, Inaugural Address, 1876, http://webapps.jhu.edu/jhuniverse/information_about_hopkins/about_jhu/daniel_coit_gilman/ (accessed June 2013). Subsequent quotations from Gilman are from this source.

21. Julie Reuben, *The Making of the Modern University: Intellectual Transformation and the Marginalization of Morality* (Chicago: University of Chicago Press, 1996), 11.

22. Charles W. Eliot, "The Aims of Higher Education" (1891), quoted by Reuben, 82.

23. Charles Eliot, "Inaugural Address," in *Addresses at the Inauguration of Charles William Eliot as President of Harvard College* (Cambridge, Mass.: Sever and Francis, 1869), 31.

24. The quotations from James in this paragraph are from *Talks to Teachers on Psychology: And to Students on Some of Life's Ideals* (Rockville, Md.: Arc Manor, 2008), 25–26.

25. See Robert L. Geiger, "The Ten Generations of American Higher Education," in *American Higher Education in the Twenty-first Century: Social, Political and Economic Challenges*, 3rd ed., ed. Philip G. Altbach, Patricia J. Gumport, and Robert O. Berdahl (Baltimore: Johns Hopkins University Press, 2011), 51.

26. Barbara Miller Solomon, *In the Company of Educated Women: A History of Women and Higher Education in America* (New Haven: Yale University Press, 1985), 31.

27. Quoted in ibid., 49.

28. Ibid., 83.

29. M. Carey Thomas, "Should the Higher Education of Women Differ from That of Men?" *Educational Review* 21 (1901). The quotation is from the final paragraph of the essay. The essay begins with a strong, humorous defense of women's professional education: "So long as men and women are to compete together, and associate together, in

their professional life, women's preparation for the same profession cannot safely differ from men's." Thomas helped establish the medical school at Johns Hopkins University.

30. Frederick Rudolph put it this way in his *The American College and University: A History* (New York: Vintage, 1962): "A curriculum, a library, a faculty, and students are not enough to make a college. It is an adherence to the residential scheme of things . . . permeated by paternalism. It is what every American college has had or consciously rejected or lost or sought to recapture. It is William Tecumseh Sherman promising to be a father to an entire student body; it is comfort and full tobacco jars in a Princeton dormitory; in an urban university it is counselors helping the socially inept to overcome their weaknesses" (86). Quoted by Lester F. Goodchild, "Transformations of the American College Ideal: Six Historic Ways of Learning," *New Directions for Higher Education*, no. 105 (Spring 1999): 9–10.

31. See Reuben, 253.

32. Geiger, 58.

33. Reuben, chap. 7, especially 215–29.

34. Quoted in Goodchild, 15–16.

35. Menand, *Marketplace*, 31.

36. Ibid., 34. See also Carnochan, 76.

37. *General Education in a Free Society: Report of the Harvard Committee*, with an introduction by James Bryant Conant (Cambridge, Mass.: Harvard University Press, 1950), 4, http://archive.org/stream/generaleducation032440mbp/generaleducation032440mbp_djvu.txt (accessed June 2013). Subsequent references to this work are given parenthetically in the text.

38. James Bryant Conant, "Education for a Classless Society: The Jeffersonian Tradition," *Atlantic Monthly*, May 1940, http://www.theatlantic.com/past/docs/issues/95sep/ets/edcla.htm (accessed July 2013); and "Wanted: American Radicals," *Atlantic Monthly*, May 1943, http://www.theatlantic.com/past/docs/issues/95sep/ets/radical.htm (accessed July 2013).

39. It's for this reason that Nicholas Lehman has recently called Conant one of the founders of our contemporary model of meritocracy: Nicholas Lehman, *The Big Test: The Secret History of the American Meritocracy*

(New York: Farrar, Straus and Giroux, 1999), 5–8. See also the interview with Lehman in the *Atlantic*, October 7, 1999, http://www.theatlantic.com/past/docs/unbound/interviews/ba991007.htm (accessed July 2013).

40. Conant also was a champion of scholarships at Harvard for students with great aptitude but few financial resources. Menand, *Marketplace*, 38.

41. The distortions of the message of the *Red Book* are well documented by historians of education. See, for example, Phyllis Keller, *Getting at the Core: Curricular Reform at Harvard* (Cambridge, Mass.: Harvard University Press, 1982), 17. Quoted in Menand, *Marketplace*, 43, and in Harvard's *Report of the Committee on General Education* (Cambridge, Mass.: Harvard University Press, 2005). Menand was a member of the 2005 committee.

42. Geiger, 60.

43. Ibid., 60–61.

44. Christopher Jencks, "Introduction to the 2002 Edition," in Christopher Jencks and David Reisman, *The Academic Revolution* (New Brunswick, N.J.: Transaction, 2002), xii. He notes that "college teachers hardly ever visit one another's classrooms, and when they do, they rarely say anything critical. As a result, college teaching has never been professionalized in the way research has."

45. *The Study of Education at Stanford: A Report to the University* (1968), 1:3, 2:10, cited by Carnochan, 97.

46. Ibid., 2:24. 1:14. See Carnochan, 97–98.

47. Alan Bloom, *The Closing of the American Mind* (New York: Simon and Schuster, 1987), 252.

48. Ibid., 239.

49. Ibid., 382.

50. David Rieff, "The Colonel and the Professor," *Times Literary Supplement*, September 4, 1987, 950, 960.

51. Carnochan, 103–6.

52. See Kimball; and Orrill.

53. See Lauren Weber, "Do Too Many Young People Go to College?" *Wall Street Journal*, June 21, 2012, http://online.wsj.com/article/SB10001424052970203960804577239253121093694.html (accessed June 2013).

54. See Peter Wood, "Helium, Part II," a blog at *Chronicle of Higher Education*, July 23, 2012. http://chronicle.com/blogs/innovations/ helium-part-2/33693. Also "Unfashionable Ideas," July 20, 2012, at the website of the National Association of Scholars, http://www.nas.org/articles/unfashionable_ideas (accessed July 2013).

55. Lumina Foundation website: http://www.luminafoundation.org/ about_us/ (accessed July 2013).

56. Jamie P. Merisotis, "The Difference Makers: Adult Students and Achieving Goal 2025," 2011, http://www.luminafoundation.org/about_ us/president/speeches/2011–11–03-the_difference_makers-adult_students_and_achieving_goal_2025.html (accessed July 2013).

57. Jamie P. Merisotis, "It's the Learning, Stupid," lecture at Claremont Graduate University, 2009, http://www.luminafoundation.org/about_us/ president/speeches/2009–10–14.html (accessed July 2013).

58. See aacu.org, especially the LEAP program. I am a trustee of the AAC&U.

59. This paragraph draws on "Degree Qualifications Profile" from the Lumina Foundation website: http://www.luminafoundation.org/?s= %22Degree+Profile%22&x=0&y=0 (accessed July 2013). See also the work of the American Association of Colleges and Universities on liberal education "as a nation goes to college": http://www.aacu.org/resources/liberaleducation/index.cfm (accessed July 2013).

60. See Thiel's comments in the *National Review*, January 20, 2011, "Back to the Future with Peter Thiel," http://www.nationalreview.com/articles/257531/back-future-peter-thiel-interview?pg=3 (accessed July 2013).

61. This is a recurrent theme in contemporary discourse about higher education. See Craig Brandon, *The Five-Year Party: How Colleges Have Given Up on Educating Your Child and What You Can Do about It* (New York: BenBella Books, 2010); and the more scholarly book by Richard Arnum and Josipa Roksa, *Academically Adrift: Limited Learning on College Campuses* (Chicago: University of Chicago Press, 2013).

62. See Thiel's comments.

63. See http://www.thielfellowship.org/ (accessed July 2013).

64. http://thielfoundation.org/index.php?option=com_content&view= article&id=33:peter-thiel-announces-2012-class-of-20-under-20-thiel-fellows&catid=1:commentary&Itemid=16 (accessed July 2013).

65. http://www.thielfellowship.org/become-a-fellow/faq/ (accessed July 2013).

66. Thiel.

67. Menand, *Marketplace*, 52.

68. Ibid.

69. Delbanco, 85.

70. Menand, *Marketplace*, 55.

71. Victor E. Ferrall Jr., *Liberal Arts at the Brink* (Cambridge, Mass.: Harvard University Press, 2011), 47. Ferrall is quoting GDA Integrated Services, *Three Cues* newsletter, 2007, www.dehne.com.

4.

RESHAPING OURSELVES AND OUR SOCIETIES

1. *The Philosophy of John Dewey*, ed. John J. McDermott (Chicago: University of Chicago Press, 1973), 464. In this chapter, all page citations are from this volume.

2. John Dewey, "Education vs. Trade Training," quoted in Robert B. Westbrook, *John Dewey and American Democracy* (Ithaca: Cornell University Press, 1991), 176. Westbrook's account of Dewey's objections to narrowly vocational education is incisive.

3. James T. Kloppenberg, "Pragmatism and the Practice of History: From Turner and Du Bois to Today," *Metaphilosophy* 35 (2004): 202–25.

4. John Dewey, "The Function of the Liberal Arts College in a Democratic Society: The Problem of the Liberal Arts College," *American Scholar* 13, no. 4 (1944): 391–93.

5. Kloppenberg, 213.

6. E. D. Hirsch, "Why General Knowledge Should Be a Goal of Education," *Common Knowledge* 11 (1998): 14–16; see http://www.coreknowledge.org.

7. Martha Nussbaum, *Not for Profit: Why Democracy Needs the Humanities* (Princeton: Princeton University Press, 2010), 60.

8. Ibid., 65. Nussbaum is quoting Dewey, *The Child and the Curriculum: Including the School and Society* (New York: Cosimo, 2010), 15.

9. Richard Rorty, "Education as Socialization and as Individualization" in *Philosophy and Social Hope* (New York: Penguin, 1999), 114–26.

10. See Edward Glasser, *An Experiment in the Development of Critical Thinking* (New York: Teachers College Press, 1941); and Robert Ennis, "A Concept of Critical Thinking," *Harvard Educational Review* 32 (1962): 82–111. See also http://www.criticalthinking.org/pages/defining-critical-thinking/766 (accessed July 2013).

11. See Robert Pippin, "Natural and Normative," *Daedalus* 138 (2009): 35–43; Ruth Leys, "The Turn to Affect: A Critique," *Critical Inquiry* 37 (2011): 434–72; Curtus White, *The Science Delusion: Asking the Big Questions in a Culture of Easy Answers* (New York: Melville House, 2013).

12. "Statement to the Conference on the Curriculum for the College of Liberal Arts," cited by Robert Orrill in "An End to Mourning: Liberal Education in Contemporary America," in Bruce Kimball, *The Condition of American Liberal Education: Pragmatism and a Changing Tradition*, ed. Robert Orrill (New York: College Board, 1995), xvii.

13. See the introduction to this book and Kimball's excellent *Condition of American Liberal Education*.

14. William James, "On a Certain Blindness," in *Writings of William James*, 630.

Index

Index

relevance of liberal education
(*continued*)
See also citizenship and
education; freedom and
education
religion and education: in the
18th century, 22, 23, 29, 31,
199(n12); denominational
institutions, 113, 116;
free inquiry and, 112;
uncoupling of, 107,
109–10, 113
Renouvier, Charles, 87
required courses, 138
research universities: consensus
regarding "permanent
questions" lost, 140–41;
evolution of higher
education dominated, 162;
German model, 74–75,
106–7, 109, 115; Gilman on,
109–11; Harvard transformed
into, 72; relationship to
undergraduate studies,
111–12; research standards,
136; scholar-teacher model,
110; specialization and
compartmentalization,
113–15, 133–35; student-
teacher relationships,
136–37. *See also* universities
and colleges; *and specific
institutions*

residential college experience,
19–20, 121, 122–24, 146,
155, 206(n30)
rhetorical tradition, 3–4, 5
Rieff, David, 143
Roosevelt, Theodore, 9, 80
Rorty, Richard: liberal
education championed, 10;
on liberal learning and
citizenship, 180–81;
"philosopher as referee"
deconstructed, 176–78,
188; on primary and
secondary education, 178–79;
on self-transformation
through liberal education,
18, 181, 193–94; spectatorial
theoretical Left criticized,
186
rote learning: antidotes, 179,
192; Emerson's criticism of,
50–51, 58–59; Jefferson
opposed to, 51; reducing,
103, 159
Royce, Josiah, 90
Rudolph, Frederick, 206(n30)
Rush, Benjamin, 28, 36,
199(n12)

SAT (Scholastic Aptitude
Test), 130
scholar-teacher model, 110.
See also research universities

Index

sciences: ascendancy, 125; impact on higher education, 4; Jefferson's emphasis on, 31–32, 33; methodologies widely adopted, 125; principles and methodology needed in jobs, 153; research universities' focus on, 107 (*see also* research universities)

secondary education: general education in, 132; high school graduation rates, 125; socialization the main function of, 178; vocational learning in, 164

selectivity, 16, 120–21, 135

self-discovery: conformity a threat to, 55–56; Dewey on, 7; educational freedom and, 34–35; Emerson on, 47; in Jefferson's educational model, 34, 59; liberal education as means toward, 17; through study of literature, 126

"Self-Reliance" (Emerson), 48, 54–59

service learning, 82

"Silence Dogood" letters, 95–96

skepticism, 4, 183. *See also* critical thinking; free inquiry; inquiry

slavery, 37–44. *See also* African Americans

Smith College, 78, 117

social responsibility and education, 68–71, 84–85. *See also* citizenship and education

specialization: dangers of overspecialization, 114–15; dangers of specialized education, 132–33, 190; by faculty, 121–23, 132, 133–36, 157; liberal education as foundation for, 105, 106, 110–12, 146; liberal/general education as counterbalance, 132–33; transcending, 133–34. *See also* research universities

St. John's College, 138

standardized testing, 179

state universities. *See* public universities; universities and colleges

Stevenson, Robert Louis, 90

student debt, 2, 20, 146. *See also* college costs

students: capacity for study, 58; careerism, 1, 163 (*see also* monetization of education); choice of path of study, 6, 34, 72–73, 104, 110, 137–39, 150, 191 (*see also* elective

Index